# *A Bedouin Boyhood*

# A Bedouin Boyhood

ISAAK DIQS

GEORGE ALLEN & UNWIN LTD
London

UNIVERSE BOOKS
New York

George Allen & Unwin (Publishers) Ltd,
40 Museum Street, London WC1A 1LU, UK

George Allen & Unwin (Publishers) Ltd,
Park Lane, Hemel Hempstead, Herts HP2 4TE, UK

George Allen & Unwin Australia Pty Ltd,
8 Napier Street, North Sydney, NSW 2060, Australia

First published in 1967
Second impression 1984

Published in the United States of America in 1983
by Universe Books
381 Park Avenue South, New York, N.Y. 10016

83  84  85  86  87  /  10  9  8  7  6  5  4  3  2  1

Library of Congress Cataloging in Publication Data

Diqs, Isaak, 1938-
    A Bedouin boyhood.

    Reprint. Originally published: New York: Praeger,
1969, c1967.
    1. Bedouins.  2. Diqs, Isaak, 1938- .  3. Bedouins—
Biography.  I. Title.
DS36.9.B4D56 1983     956.94 '04 '0924 [B]     83-10451
ISBN 0-87663-430-7

Printed in the United States of America

*To all of my people*
*driven from their land*

◆◆

# CONTENTS

# AUTHOR'S NOTE

This book is true. I have written it in English, which is neither my native language nor perfectly known to me. Nevertheless I am told by at least one person competent to know that here I have said no more and no less than I mean.

I am grateful to the Editor of *The Times* for permission to reproduce as the first chapter my very first writing, which was published as the turnover article in *The Times* of 13 March 1965. I must also express my thanks to Mr. Robert Seeds, of the English Department, Riyadh University, for his special mixture of encouragement, vituperation and skill, which enabled me to start, continue and complete this book of recollections, reflections and, it may or may not be, of judgment.

I.D.

# Glossary

DONUM — Originally, the area of land that a farmer could plow in one day; today, the unit means precisely 0.22 acre.

GADEER — The water or stream within a wadi.

HAJ — A title given to an adult who has made the pilgrimage to Mecca, the Muslim holy city. The title demands respect, but, for the bedouins, it has more social than religious significance.

HOWDAH — A seat or pavilion, generally covered, carried on the back of a camel.

MATTOCK — A hoelike instrument used for digging.

MUKHTAR — An elected village headman; literally, "chosen one."

PANNIER — A large wicker basket carried on the back or side of a horse.

PILLION — A pad or cushion placed behind a man's saddle, chiefly for a woman to ride on.

RAMADAN — The ninth month of the Muslim calendar, in which it is believed the Prophet Muhammad received his divine revelation. Muslims throughout the world celebrate these thirty days by fasting from sunrise to sunset, and end each day's abstinence with a lavish meal. The month terminates with a festival or feast, during which children are given pocket money and are allowed to visit friends without parental supervision. A spirit of charity pervades the celebrations.

WADI — A valley or ravine through which a stream flows. To a bedouin, the *wadi* has the connotation of one's home or a meeting place, and the word conveys a sense of protection.

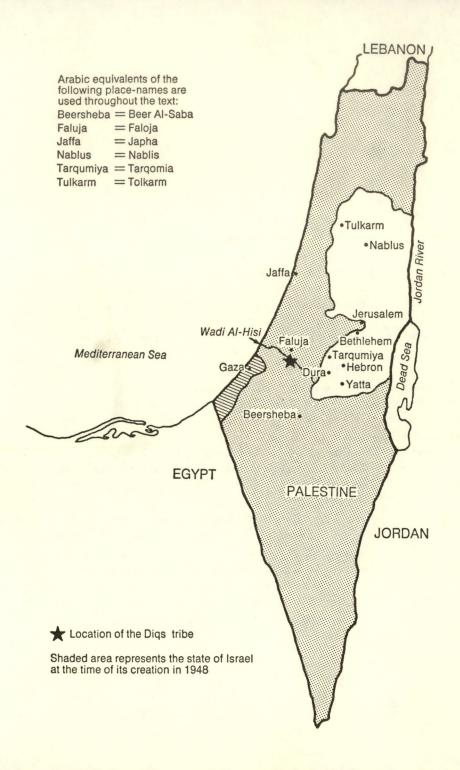

Arabic equivalents of the
following place-names are
used throughout the text:
Beersheba = Beer Al-Saba
Faluja    = Faloja
Jaffa     = Japha
Nablus    = Nablis
Tarqumiya = Tarqomia
Tulkarm   = Tolkarm

LEBANON

•Tulkarm

•Nablus

Jaffa•

Jerusalem

Wadi Al-Hisi

Faluja•

Bethlehem

•Tarqumiya

Gaza•

•Hebron

Dura•

•Yatta

Mediterranean Sea

Beersheba•

Jordan River

Dead Sea

EGYPT

PALESTINE

JORDAN

★ Location of the Diqs tribe

Shaded area represents the state of Israel
at the time of its creation in 1948

# CHAPTER 1

## The Small Cow-herd

WHEN I used to keep the sheep on the slopes of Wadi Al-Hisi, our tribe was not in need of going from one place to another, because both the climate and soil were good. The grandfathers were proud that they did not leave that good *wadi* because it was enough to keep them and their animals. They did not know about the outside world, except on Thursdays when men and women used to go to the neighbouring village to buy some necessities. They used to go there early in the morning, riding on horses and camels. Old men in the tribe used to foretell the weather, and most times they were right.

There was only one school, with four classes. I had spent four years there before in free time taking part of the family's responsibilities by keeping our sheep.

Thus was the situation of our tribe, when my mother one spring morning awakened me because all the shepherds were leaving. I got up and took the food she had prepared for me. I flapped my robe at the sheep to tell them to follow me, and left the tents among the bleating of sheep and lowing of cows. These sounds were mixed with the voices of the shepherds calling to each other. As I went farther I heard nothing but the faint musical sound of the *mihbash* being used for grinding the coffee. My sheep were following me, passing on the dewy grass and awakening the small birds which flew up in the misty air to sing their momentarily happy songs. The sun was just rising, sending its golden threads among the tops of the hills and scattering the mist which was mixed with the smoke that came from the tents.

13

I do not know why we used to go towards the east in the morning. It may be because we liked to feel the warmth of the sun.

I looked backward and saw my cousin, Shehadi, a small boy about twelve years old, as old as me, driving his cows with his heavy stick in his hand. I expected him to follow, because we used to go together every day, but that day he waved to me and went to the southern hills. We feared those hills, because it was said that a battle had taken place there and ghosts of the killed soldiers used to appear there at night. Those hills were completely deserted, except for lovers, who made their appointments there.

I reached a green hill and stayed there, looking at my sheep eating the grass and listening to a shepherd playing on his pipe on the opposite hill. I spent most of the day near the deserted spring from which the animals used to drink in summer. I was glad to see my sheep eating while the small wagtails were jumping in the shade of the sheep.

When the sun began to send its rays towards the west, my sheep began to look at me as if they were telling me that it was time for going home. So I walked in front of them while they followed me, at first in a slow movement, still eating. As the sun went down they came closer, and the one which had the bell on her neck came first and was followed by the others. I passed by the cowherds, who had to stay for about two hours after sunset because cows used to eat much after sunset. That was a suitable time for lovers to meet unseen by people, because the custom was that shepherds and cow-herds were from both sexes.

When I came near to the tents I could see the smoke, which rose till it was mixed with the falling night. There was a complete silence. Every mother or wife was preparing the main meal, for the whole family could not gather except at night. That silence did not last for a long time, because the sheep were coming from everywhere. When they came they were bleating and running to meet their small lambs. I used to enjoy the scene of a small lamb missing his mother and pushing his head at the udder of any ewe, then leaving her quickly when revealed as a stranger. My small brother ran with the lambs to meet me and asked for a new-born lamb because the day before I had brought him one.

Mothers, wives and sisters began to milk the sheep, and fathers took a look at their animals. The cows arrived just after those jobs were finished, and they in their turn were milked.

When all work was done, our family sat around our humble meal. Then my father left us to join the other men in the *Shik*, the tent where men sat together to spend their spare time in discussing their daily problems or, when they had none, listening to the tribe's bard telling, to the tunes of his *rababah*, the past's glorious days. In spite of my father's warning, I used not to go to bed unless I heard the story of the poet. I remember how my father found me one night asleep in a corner of the *Shik*.

As the night went on, the silence became deeper except for the voice of the one-stringed fiddle and some cicadas to be heard when one went outside the tent. Suddenly the silence was broken by the voice of my aunt calling for my uncle from the women's part of the tent: 'Oh Taleb, you are listening and amusing yourself while our boy is lost. Shehadi has not come yet.'

My uncle was too proud to show his anxiety, so he waited for a while, then went out. An old man, who was sitting beside the fire, drew slow lines on the sand with the end of his long pipe and pronounced that it was shameful for such young men to stay while a small boy of the tribe had not come yet. I did not pay attention to the people around me because I was still thinking of the hero's fate. When I came back to my senses I found myself alone with other small children around the dying fire.

Some of the men returned, but without finding Shehadi. I could hear someone calling: 'Have you found the boy?' The answer came: 'No, we have not.'

I knew where Shehadi had gone, but I was afraid to tell them because they would reproach me for not having told them before. But in spite of that fear I told my elder brother, who announced what I said, and told me to mount behind him so as to show him the way Shehadi had taken. Soon he was followed by many men and women. Along the way I imagined Shehadi among those hills attacked by the terrible ghosts of the dead soldiers.

As we went farther, the people came closer, because they thought that I could tell the exact place and everyone wanted to be the first to find the boy and his cows. My uncle became very anxious: I knew that because he was completely silent.

When we reached the place where it was said that the battle

had taken place, my brother spurred the horse, which broke into a quick canter. Then the horse stopped suddenly, pricking his ears, and my brother shouted: 'Here are the cows.' And he shouted more loudly: 'Shehadi!'

But no one replied. To our surprise we saw the cows stretching their necks and breathing softly, sweetly, along with the odour of the dewy flowers. Among them, encircled, was a small heap of cloth.

My brother dismounted and ran quickly and awakened Shehadi. The men and women stood silent and were astonished that the cows had not left the boy and gone home as was their habit. We went back, following the cows which knew their way home.

In the morning we began a new day and Shehadi passed by me. He was closer to his cows and with no stick in his hand.

That was the kind of life we led where troubles ended by nightfall and hopes renewed with the sunrise. It was a simple life, but it was interesting because we saw new things daily.

How far are we from that life? Nineteen, as years go. But cows now will fear Shehadi because he has become a skilled worker at stone-crushing and cement-mixing machines—he is noisy, white-powdered, weird. And how far am I from that life? Now that I am bespectacled, blue-suited, smart—now that I, Isaak ibn-Abdulaziz Al-Diqs, have a fair-sized desk at the Ministry and expect quite soon to move to a really fine desk with many empty trays for important papers—well, I am far from my beginnings and only sometimes just a little nostalgic of soul.

# CHAPTER 2

## *Bin Rizk, a Thief*

A FEW miles to the western side of Wadi Al-Hisi our tribe had decided one year to spend winter time. So late in autumn they set up their tents on a plain surrounded by hills on three sides—west, north and south. They used to do this every year so as to avoid the strong south-westerly wind. Special tents were made as was usual in that season. They were well made, so no rain could get through. Different kinds of wood were prepared, near every tent one could see a big heap of wood ready for the winter fire.

It was the time of a short rest for the people, because after a few days they would begin ploughing the land and sowing their seeds. The simple equipment was already prepared, because it was supposed to be a good year. Enough rain would come, and the good evidence for that was the early appearance of *hitan*, a kind of autumn flower which used to be considered a true barometer: if these flowers appeared early, then the rain would come early. One could see some of them in white and pink groups around the crowded tents. Many of them were growing on both sides of the road that came from Wadi Al-Hisi, passed near the tribe and led to the few houses built for keeping the harvest and animal-fodder, and used sometimes for people who went to them in hard winters.

It was one night of that part of the year, when a big group of men were sitting in the *Shik*, the biggest tent in the tribe. There was no certain subject to be discussed, so many topics were dealt with and many things were said. The weather was expected to be

17

good, that side of the tribe's land would be ploughed and that one would be left for grazing. Such was the talk.

This varied and uncontrolled talk went on till cut by Haj Ibrahim, an old man, saying, 'The future is out of our control, but, God willing, you will find enough land for your camels to plough, and even for Abu Jaber's new red tractor to plough, and for your animals to eat. Stop these discussions! Come, Ziadi, and please us with your *rababah*! Tell us about the story of Nimr Aladwan and his faithful wife!'

This idea was clearly applauded by all the people, because they became silent except for those who insisted upon Ziadi making his *rababah* taut in the heat of the fading fire. Ziadi was willing to play, because it was a suitable time since he knew that some women guests were in the women's part of the tent. So it was a good opportunity for him and should not be missed.

The night went on, with Ziadi playing cleverly on his *rababah* and sending up his sighs at the misfortunes of that faithful woman whose story he sang. He was not interrupted, except when he had to heat his one-stringed fiddle to tighten it or to drink a cup of coffee given by an admiring young man who sat near the hearth for serving the coffee. A few men left, but the majority stayed there till the end of the story. The fire had already expired and the rest of the coffee become cold. A few minutes later, the *Shik* was empty except for the dog which was waiting in a corner till the men went outside, and then came and curved itself in the ashes of the dead fire.

Salim, one of the young men, left the *Shik* a few minutes after his father. Their tent was the last one on the northern side of the tribe. They were just three persons living in the tent—himself, Salamah his old father, and Nafleh his mother. Ali, his elder brother, had married not long before and left them to live in a separate tent, but not far from them. Their tent was divided into three parts. Two were the women's, where his parents lived, and the third was where Salim used to sleep at night and to receive his friends from the tribe, because any outsiders, friends or not, had of course to go to the *Shik*. Between his room and the others there was a long slab of wood raised upon four wooden legs. Their cushions and wool-stuffed quilts were put on that long piece of wood. Under it there were many trifles—some old pots, an old *mihbash* no longer fit for grinding the coffee, and many small cases. When Salim entered his part of the tent, he found that his father had already slept. It was nearly midnight, so he laid himself on the bed which his mother had prepared for him in the evening and soon he was asleep.

'Salim! A thief, a thief, Salim!' Salim was awakened by the excited calling of his father. But he was confused, he did not know where he should go, and without thinking he went from the back of the tent.

'Where is he, father?' shouted Salim. 'He is still in the tent,' Salamah said. Before Salim could come back, he heard a movement under the table and saw a ghost pass by his side like an arrow.

'Here he is! Follow me, father,' Salim shouted, as he ran behind the thief. At that moment all the tribe were awakened by the shouts of Salamah and his son. The shouts for help were heard everywhere. Men and women, old and young, even children, joined the pursuit. All supposed that the thief would take the northern direction because the tent was in the north, and they went in that direction, with everyone thinking that the other was sure that the thief was in front of them.

But the thief, followed only by Salim and his father, made for the western side where there was a gully about eight hundred yards away from Salamah's tent. Salamah was old, so he could not keep close to his son, who kept on at the same distance from the thief. Salim was about to catch the thief when the thief fell down, and Salim because of his great speed fell also and landed in front of the thief. Before he could stand up, the thief had already jumped up and run off very quickly.

'Follow him before he reaches the gully,' Salim heard his father urging. But it was too late, because the thief had already thrown himself into the gully, which was about four yards deep. Salim knew that the gully was deep, but he had no choice at the moment because he was too close to the thief. So before the thief could raise himself Salim had already fallen upon him, and immediately began to hit him on the head with his fist.

Salim heard his father calling, 'Don't follow him! Leave him, he may be armed!' So he took the hands of the thief, whose face was to the ground, and put his knees upon them so as to prevent him from using any weapon he might have. Before the father had reached the edge of the gully, before he could call again to his son, Salamah heard the sounds of blows and the thief asking for mercy. He shouted, 'Long live Salim! But, Salim, be careful of him, keep his hands away from anything.' Then he shouted at large, 'O men! O men! Salim has caught him!'

The old man was unable to get down because the gully was too deep for him to do so, so he kept running up and down and calling to the people, who came to the gully running and shouting *'Farhak! Farhak!'* the word usually said when answering a call for help. Minutes later most of the tribe were either in the gully or at its edges. The name 'Salim' was repeated by everyone with great admiration.

'Now you are my son—I am proud of you,' Salamah said as Salim came from the gully driving the thief, whose hands were tied by his scarf at his back. Everyone was jostling the other so as to see the thief, but because it was dark few people could see him well. The crowd reached the tents in a celebration, and the thief was pushed into the *Shik*. Soon the fire was lighted. One could see the great crowd of people—men, children, some old men—and even some young women peering through the few holes in the tent.

Among that crowd was the thief, a black middle-aged man with small eyes, big nose and curly hair now disshevelled. There was a small wound, which might have been caused by his fall or by the nails of Salim. On his feet there were socks tied with string so as to deceive any trackers, though their encumbrance had in fact helped Salim to catch him.

He was casting his eyes down and sometimes looking at the burning fire. He might be thinking of his fate. It seemed that he did not know anyone of the people present, and no one seemed to know him. It happens sometimes that one stops thinking when one completely despairs of finding a solution, and that might have happened to the thief. He sat completely silent, as if he were put apart from life and the events taking place by his side.

Salim was sitting beside him, and the people turned their faces from the thief to Salim. Before that night most of the people—and even Salamah—had looked on Salim as a still young boy and not worthy of getting Sabha, one of the most beautiful girls of the tribe, as wife. But that night everything was changed, and Salim felt that, was sure of it, so he tried to hide his feelings and to regard the event as if it were usual. Yet in spite of himself he stole some looks backward and to both sides, hoping to see Sabha—but he could not, because of the great crowd of people and because of the darkness outside.

'Which tribe are you from?' Haj Ibrahim asked the thief, who neither moved nor spoke. The question was repeated by that old, respected man, while the other men held their breath so as to learn the thief's tribe. But again the thief did not answer.

'Don't be stubborn!' a young man said, 'We know how to make angry camels yield and the wild horses become domestic as lambs. Tell us your name and your tribe's.'

'I am Bin Rizk,' he said in a rough voice.

All the people were astonished as they heard 'Bin Rizk'. He was the cleverest and most famous thief. The trackers knew him well, but usually did not tell about him—because they were either afraid of him or taking his part—though some of the trackers were honest to the degree that they told about him more than once. Soon 'Bin Rizk' was being repeated by everyone there and all the people knew that Salim had caught the most dangerous thief. The small children could not believe that they were looking at the man about whom they were told a lot by their grandmothers near the fire before going to bed. They came nearer and gazed at him: he was a man like anyone in the tribe, even was more like Mubark, a very pleasant and kind man in the tribe.

At first the children were too excited and afraid to come very near him, though they saw that his hands were tied and his feet shackled with a camel's hobble. Even when they came near they were still afraid that he, perhaps, would break his bonds and plunge off. But, because of the burning fire which changed the dark night to a shining part of the day and of the great crowd of people, they were encouraged to the extent that one of them, Mansur, a naughty small boy, poked him with a long stick he had in his hand.

The thief did not turn his face, it might be because he did not feel the touch of the stick or because he had been suddenly struck by the idea that they would give him to the policemen in the neighbouring village. Indeed, many people were applauding this idea, and Hussein, the Sheikh of the tribe, said : 'Keep him till the morning, and then Taleb will go to Al-Faloja and tell the police-station, which will send and take him to prison.' Bin Rizk did not make any gesture or ask any mercy : he was still silent as if the matter did not concern him. Some people, even, said afterwards that they had seen a faint sarcasm on the features of his black face.

'No, my brother,' said Haj Ibrahim, who was looking into his empty cup of coffee as if to see the future. Then he put the cup down on the old silver tray and went on, 'I know the Sheikh of Bin Rizk's tribe and some of the other old men. I have been there more than once. They are good and generous people. I know that they do not agree with this evil man's work. I suggest that it is better to send for some of their old men to come and take away this thief.'

Haj Ibrahim was well-known as the best judge in all the Al-Jubarat tribes, and highly respected by the people of his tribe and the others, so the crowd became silent and seemed to be convinced by this strange suggestion. But Bin Rizk was shocked as if he had been stung, and for the first time his likeness to a statue vanished. He followed Haj Ibrahim's speech word by word and then said in a softer tone, 'Do not call for any of them. Send me anywhere, but do not let even one of my tribe see me in such a situation. Kill me—be done with it—kill me !' The greatest shame for a thief was to be arrested, and it was worse if some of his own tribe saw him—he would pass on his shame to all of his tribe.

The small children now took courage to prick him with thorns, and some naughty ones went further and pricked him with pins. They did that unseen by the old men, who noticed it from the movements of Bin Rizk. He looked at Haj Ibrahim as if he were asking him to stop the boys' actions. Haj Ibrahim responded to Bin Rizk's begging eyes and shouted : 'Stop, boys, don't be cowards ! What will the bedouins say if they hear that we have insulted our prisoner?' The small boys were affected by the old man's words, and they did not come again after Salim had pushed them back.

The fire went on burning that night. Few people could sleep. Morning coffee was made earlier than usual. The small children found it a good opportunity to enjoy playing at that time when all the people were, strangely, awake. The shepherds, cow-herds and schoolboys did not go off early that day. They waited till they could see what would be done to Bin Rizk. But before they could come to the *Shik* they had seen a tall, robust man making his way slowly to Wadi A-Hisi. They knew that it was Bin Rizk and they understood that Haj Ibrahim had finally persuaded the people there to set the man free, and had even given him one of his own scarves to replace his torn one.

Life went on and ten years passed. Salim became famous and many girls wished him for husband, but he married Sabha and got two beautiful daughters. Every year was better than the one before. People were affected by the progress of life. Tractors were seen turning the face of the good soil. Some wells were dug and some fruit-gardens were planted—grapes, figs and citrus-trees became familiar to our tribe, and some of the bedouins became specialized in that way of life.

But cows, sheep and horses were still there. They were dear to the people, and they were accustomed to seeing them in front of their tents or their newly-built houses, even if they made a fair fortune from those new methods. The school became no longer enough for the great number of boys, so three other schools were established and most of the boys used to go to the neighbouring villages after spending six years in these three elementary schools. People no more found enough time to sit together for talking, except at nights. The people preferred to stay near their estates, so one could see no longer that great number of tents, but here and there, on the green hills, one could see the newly-built houses. Every four or five stood together and near them there were still some tents, especially in spring time when it was very refreshing to stay in a tent in green fields and among growing things.

It was one day at that time of year when a group of men could be seen walking behind a thin, tall man who, from time to time, bent down. He was Hassan, the tracker of our tribe and the most famous one in all the neighbouring tribes. It was known that the jewellery of Sarah, Haj Ibrahim's daughter, had been stolen. Hassan went down a hill, then he returned upwards. He did that twice and at last he took his way and disappeared beyond the hills, followed by the group of men who grew in number as they wound on through the tribal lands.

The trail continued for two days. Sometimes Hassan seemed happy, and sometimes the marks of despair appeared on his face. The followers had nothing at all to do but to look at Hassan's face.

Before sunset of the next day they were happy, because the footprints were clear and Hassan followed them quickly and told the people that he hoped to find the thief very soon. But shortly his hope disappeared, when he came to a rocky place where even the soil was hard. In vain he tried to get out of that place : the footprints ended there and he was unable to follow them out. The sun was sinking and it was useless to stay anymore.

There was a neighbouring tribe, so they decided to spend their night as the tribe's guests. They were welcomed, their horses were tied and their food was prepared. After eating and drinking coffee together, an old man asked them about their aim, because they were unknown young men. Taleb, Haj Ibrahim's son, began to tell their story, beginning it by introducing himself and his friends. While he was telling his story, all the men in the *Shik* were attentive. Even in one of the great tent's corners an old, dark man, grey-bearded, followed Taleb's speech with clear attention, though he left the *Shik* before the end of the narrative.

The Sheikh of the tribe expressed his sorrow and said that it was strange, because for many years they had heard nothing of robbery. He promised to send some of his men in the morning to help them in their search.

In March people were accustomed to have sun on one day and rain on the next, so it was not strange when Hassan and his group were awakened by the fall of heavy rain. They knew that it was pointless to try now to follow a trail, so they decided to go back home. They thanked the Sheikh of the tribe and made for home, slowly and with despairing steps. On their way home they passed near an old, dark man. They were about to ask him if by chance he had seen a thief, but realized it would be useless and went on.

Before they could reach the tents they were met by some small children, who came helter-skelter to tell them that the stolen jewels had been found—in front of Sarah's own tent, wrapped in an old white scarf. Hassan did not wait to learn more, but ran to the place where the scarf had been found. He cast around in a half-circle, then went about two yards forward and shouted : 'It was the thief himself who returned them.'

Many years now have passed, but Salim, sometimes, when he is persistently asked, tells, with abstracted mind and his eyes looking into the unknown, the story of Bin Rizk the thief. He calls it—his words dropping distinctly, like a small scatter of pebbles to be clutched at by grandchildren—the story of Bin Rizk, the faithful and honest thief.

# CHAPTER 3

# Ramadan Fair

I saw the long road winding, sometimes among the green maize fields, and at others among the newly reaped wheat fields. It was in summer and, to be more exact, on the last Thursday of Ramadan. I had tried fasting that month : some days I was able to end the day without eating or drinking, but on others I could not resist the call of a cold drink or a cup of fresh milk. My father used to tell my mother that I was still young when she insisted upon my fasting. Few days I fasted that year, but I wished that I had fasted the whole three past weeks. I felt Ramadan to be an important month and worthy of fasting, while I was riding our white donkey along that old winding road.

I was with my aunt among a long line of people. All of them were from our tribe—men, women and some children. Some of these people were on horses, others on donkeys or camels, and a few were on foot. The people were more than on any other Thursday, because it was the last Thursday of Ramadan and one had to go shopping: to buy new clothes, shoes, sugar, rice and some sweets for the coming festival of Ramadan. I could see, while I was kicking up my white donkey, groups of people from other tribes passing along that Sultani road. They were coming in small groups along small paths, then gathered in larger ones along that old Sultani road. Some of these people were driving lambs or young bulls or maiden heifers, to sell them and then to buy with their price things necessary for the forthcoming holiday. The long line of people was broken in some places, but the whole line was moving towards the north to Al-Faloja, the nearest village.

My grandfather, Haj Ibrahim, was on his light red mare,

surrounded by many men smoking and talking. I could hear some of their talk and most of their loud laughs. Shehadi was driving a group of lambs: all of them were to be sold, except the black-headed one which was to be given as a present to Abu Husien, Haj Ibrahim's villager friend, who was accustomed to receive such a gift twice a year. I was anxious to reach the village, so sometimes I closed my eyes and began to dream of the things I expected to see in the market. I did so thinking that this would shorten the distance. I always opened my eyes to see the long line, but each time with smaller gaps.

As we came up the last hill which separated us from the village I could see the important, big village, surrounded by many great citrus-orchards and sugar-cane fields. I could also see the smoke going up to the sky from the flour-mills and the small pottery factory. The sounds of the pumps were clearly heard above the loud noise of the people inside the village. I also saw the people disappearing through the sugar-cane fields. The line of people became shorter and shorter, till we too passed through the thick plants. I understood what my brother had said to me once—that many beasts lived there because the canes were too thick to see more than one or two yards ahead.

We entered the village. I saw the children of the village playing with balls in the dusty roads. They looked at us for a while, then went on as if no one had passed. I saw also some of the girls and women of the village. They were fair and seemed to be beautiful in their long, striped dresses and with their white cloths on their heads. They looked at us too and for a while, then went inside their houses. Haj Ibrahim and his people tried to be serious, and stopped laughing when they were passing through the streets of the village. I saw some of the villagers hastening towards us.

'What are they running for?' I asked. 'They are running,' my aunt answered, 'to buy the lambs and the cows before the people can know the prices.'

I saw two of them coming towards Saleh, who got down from his horse and collected his three lambs. The shorter one of them began to feel the lambs and sometimes to lift them in his hands, testing the weight. He came to Saleh and put Saleh's hand in his, while the fat man came and put his hands around theirs. The bargaining began in a low voice, then the voices of the men

27

became louder and louder. I stopped my donkey, in spite of my aunt's calling, to see the end of that bargaining, which I thought would end in a quarrel, and I wondered why our men passed by Saleh between these two rude men without stopping.

The first man drew away his hand and left Saleh's hand in the big and hairy hand of the fat man. I heard his loud voice: 'Sell them! Two pounds for every one of such thin lambs! Sell them.' I could see Saleh trying to draw his hand away, but it seemed to be impossible. I knew that Saleh was known as one who could easily be moved. Yet he refused to sell his lambs, though the man was insisting and pressed Saleh's hand firmly. 'Let loose my hand, I say. It is a rudeness, not bargaining.' Saleh said these words and tried to reach for his waist, but before his hand could get hold of anything there the fat man had already released it, left Saleh and begun to look for another bedouin whose lambs he might buy.

I followed our people among the crowd and passed many sellers showing their goods, fruit, vegetables, cloth and many other things on wooden platters in front of their shops on both sides of the street. The market where the animals had to be sold was surrounded by wire, so all the people had to enter from one gate and go out through another. I passed through the noisy crowd to the place where I saw my grandfather's red horse standing. I found few people, so I tied my donkey to one of the empty rings and followed my aunt for shopping. While I was passing through the market I saw much of the same bargaining I had seen before. Some camels and horses were ridden by people and forced to run in front of others so as to show their ability. In the corner for donkeys I saw a young man riding his small black donkey and pricking it with a pointed stick and beating it quickly with his heels, while a group of men were laughing at the young man and his lazy donkey which refused to walk and tried more than once to go backwards in spite of the rapid beating and painful pricks of its owner. Finally the man got down from his donkey and looked at it with a great contempt.

As I left I found that I had missed my aunt. I had little money because the money for our necessities was with her. I went among the people looking carefully at every woman dressed in black. Some of these women were surprised, while others did not notice me but went on buying their small things. At last I found my aunt buying dried figs from a beautiful young girl who was standing behind a big table covered with different foodstuffs. My aunt told me to keep close to her or I should be lost again. While I was walking close behind my aunt, I saw some of the people of our tribe buying their necessities from the market. I saw too some children carrying their goods and showing them to the walking men.

An hour after noon our people began to come to the corner where their animals were to be found. Other people began to leave the place with full bags of different things. Many left before we did. We were waiting for Haj Ibrahim, and he came at last accompanied by his friend, Abu Husien, an old man with grey beard and a healthy, smiling face. I noticed how friendly he behaved towards my grandfather. He insisted on accompanying him till we came out of the village. So no one rode his animal, because Haj Ibrahim led his light red horse and led the group with his friend, Abu Husien. I had to do as the other people, so I drove my white donkey and went with the group. Everyone mounted his animal after Abu Husien had left.

I saw again the line of the returning people, but this time it was shorter than it had been in the morning. Few lambs and cows were seen. They had been left in the village. I knew their fate was to be killed, poor small lambs. The gaps in the line became wider and wider as we went on. The small paths were full of the return-ing bedouins. We passed through Wadi Al-Hisi where the animals drank. After having a short rest we left the place to some young girls who came to fill their jars with water. We passed by the tents of the Al-Rawawah tribe. I heard the cockcrows coming from the tents. Some of the dogs ran to attack the group, but, coming near and seeing the great number of people, they stopped and began to look at each other instead.

We were met by some small children. The people began to give them some of the sweets they had, because it was the custom that people coming from shopping had to give the small children some sweets. My aunt called one of these, one with wide black eyes and a woollen skull-cap on his head, worn rakishly to one side. He was looking at my aunt's hand dealing with the paper-bag which contained the dried figs. The child took them, thanked my aunt, looked at me and went away. He did not turn his head despite

29

being called by a friend, because it was shameful if he took from two people. I saw the small children, each one trying to show his piece of luck, while others ran towards the tents, perhaps to show their presents to still other people.

When we came near our own tribe we were met by the children, but everyone met his relative and those who had none were given presents by the people. In every tent there was a small meeting around the new things brought by the returning people. Clothes and shoes were tried on : some children were happy because their clothes and shoes fitted, while others were sad, and some of them were crying because, naturally, the shoes of one's brother are always better than one's own. The young girls too were examining the clothes brought back for them for the happy day, but their joy or sadness was not exposed like that of the children. The *Shik* was empty for more than half-an-hour because most of the men were at their own tents.

The days before the feast passed quickly and they were full of preparations for the long-awaited day. The feast happened to be a Thursday. Wednesday night few people slept, while most of them stayed awake till the morning. I was unable to resist the attack of sleep, so I slept at nearly midnight. Early in the morning I was awakened by the great loud sound of a huge crowd of people chanting 'God is great! God is great! Thanks be to Him! Thanks be to Him!' I washed my face, put on my new clothes and ran towards the nearby hill. I saw many horses and camels tethered near the *Shik*. A mass of people was repeating the prayers. I saw the men of our tribe with many strangers. It was a tradition that the people of the neighbouring tribes used to come to our tribe's land to pray on the two feasts.

Abu Tamaa had been leading the festal praying as long as I could remember. He was in the middle of the big human circle. The recitation stopped when Abu Tamaa turned his face towards the south—to Mecca—and began to call loudly to prayer. Quickly the people lined up in six long lines and the praying began. It lasted for about twenty minutes, then Abu Tamaa turned his face towards the people and began to preach to them and to tell them about happiness in heaven and torture in hell. The people were silent as if they were white and black stones.

When Abu Tamaa came to the end of his sermon, the people ran quickly to him to shake hands; then they turned to both my grandfathers, Sheikh Hussein who was the *sheikh* of the tribe, and his brother Haj Ibrahim, who was the recognized judge in the district and the eldest of his brothers. Many lambs were killed that day. The strangers were invited : some accepted, while others excused themselves, mounted their beasts and went off towards their tribes. At lunch time many big plates were brought to the *Shik*, where both guests and hosts ate. Then the guests left, hastily, for their tribes.

I saw that the young people, both boys and girls, were anxious to leave the tribe for Garara, where many young people from the fourteen different tribes of Al-Jubarat used to gather for singing, dancing and racing. I saw groups of girls and young men : some on their horses, while others were walking. On an elevation in that wide plain I saw a great crowd of people—men, women and children. A few horses were racing, while the young women, collected in groups, were singing songs about a strange lover who would come on his black horse and tell his girl tales of love and then take her far beyond the deserted hills. Indeed many young strangers—who might well turn out lovers—were a few yards from the waiting girls and singing and dancing to the tunes of the wooden, twin-piped *nai*. Some shots were heard as a mark of joy. Most of the horses were tired by hard, dashing riding, waiting for the suitable time when the greatest number of people would come.

The crowd became bigger and bigger as the small human groups came from all directions to that raised place. The shepherds and cow-herds brought their animals near the hill too. It was a good opportunity for single young men to see girls from other tribes. It was an old tradition : four or five girls gathered in a group and covered their heads with a very large piece of cloth under which they used to sing. If any young man was beloved by any girl he was allowed to come under that shawl, just to look at the girls and to talk with any girl he loved. Many love stories began under that shawl. I saw my brother Ibrahim getting under it. I knew that Nora, from Al-Rawawa, was one of the girls inside. She was considered to be the most beautiful girl in the district, and all the young men, in our tribe and others, were anxious to see her. Ibrahim kept his head inside the shawl for a few minutes and then he came out with a victorious smile on his face.

There were many children in their coloured clothes. They joined both the dances of men and the women singing. I entered the shawl that my brother had entered. I saw the girls' faces blushing and I recognized Nora because she was the most beautiful girl in that group. She was a little taller than the other girls, with long black and soft locks. She was also a little fairer than her friends and her eyes were not as dark as the other girls' eyes but yet had a certain charm. As she smiled, when a girl of our tribe told her that I was the brother of Ibrahim, she was beautiful really, and I realized that people were right when they said so. As I was inside, the girls praised my grandfather in a song, and I heard many shots from the men's side applauding the praise.

A small, pretty girl climbed up on the shoulders of one of these groups. She was holding in her right hand the green *qena* and she began to wave that green piece of cloth, which was fixed to a small stick. The songs became more enthusiastic. The young men hastened to their horses, and in a few minutes the Garara was beaten hard by the hoofs of the racing horses. I saw my cousin Shehdi on my grandfather's chestnut and Ibrahim on our old dun mare. Despite being old the Kbiesheh, our horse, was well-known to most of the neighbouring tribes. No horse had been able to pass her up to that time. Many people had advised my father to let her be entered in the official race, but he refused without giving a reason. My brother and my cousin were close to each other. They seemed unwilling to tire their horses because there was a serious errand awaiting them : there was little importance in that part of the racing, but much when the *qena* must be snapped from the girl's hand. The one who could get the *qena* and reach his tribe's land without being overtaken would have gained the honour, and this used to happen but once a year at the End of Ramadan Feast. Our horse had brought back the *qena* more than once in spite of its having been taken by good and fast horses.

I noticed some of the younger of the other men trying to draw my brother into a real race, but he refused and said, 'There's the true judge,' pointing confidently to the *qena*. The men smiled, except for a dark young man who seemed to be unaware of what was taking place. He was playing with the reins of his smart black mare. He looked at the Kbiesheh as my brother spurred her and set off side-by-side with my cousin. The dark young man with the black mare followed, but not so fast, so they were already returning when they met him in the middle of the racing distance. He was galloping very fast when he came back. He was leaning on his mare's neck, whose tail was curved over her back, and I heard an old man standing by my side saying, 'It is good, that black horse. It is promising and I . . . ' Before the old man could finish his sentence, the *qena* was snapped up by that dark young man who passed by like an arrow.

I heard the men and women invoking the horsemen to follow the man. Many horses followed him, and I looked for my brother but did not see him among the very fast galloping horses. The horses could hardly be seen through the dust caused by their hoofs. They disappeared in the east. The women ceased to sing and men stopped talking. It was a pause of suspense.

A few minutes passed before some of the horses returned. It became clear that the dark horseman was from Abu Jaber's tribe. The riders who returned said that Ibrahim was the only one who kept close to the bearer of the *qena* and there had been few yards between them when they disappeared behind the hills. Soon after, my cousin Shehdi returned and he told the sad news: 'Ibrahim was about to overtake the man—when he entered Abu Jaber's land.' So we lost the *qena* that year. The festival came to its end, and everyone went home as the sun was going fast towards the Mediterranean where one used to see it sink.

On the road Shehdi was asked about Ibrahim, and he answered that he had refused to come back because he was ashamed to confront his father. He had left the horse on foot despite Shehdi's trying to convince him of the uselessness of what he was doing. Before we could reach the tribe, the news had already been announced by the small children who had rushed on ahead. My father seemed to be angry. I heard Haj Ibrahim saying to him, 'It's age, my dear son. Neither the Kbiesheh nor Ibrahim is to be blamed.'

'It is impossible,' my father said passionately.

As the sun was setting the Kbiesheh came slowly from the east, white from dried sweat, and no one was on her. My father did not go to meet her while she passed in front of the *Shik* towards our tent, but he looked at her with a great sorrow and asked, 'Who is the man who snatched the *qena*?'

'He is from Abu Jaber's tribe, a young dark man on a black mare. She has three white socks and a small white star,' the old man said.

'Is it Abu Sabah's mare?' my father asked hastily. But no one could tell him the name of the horse.

Next morning, when the Kbiesheh was still eating her humble breakfast, two horsemen came from the east. One was on a white horse and the other was on the same mare which had won the honour the previous day. But he was not the same horseman : he was an old man. They were met by our people and their horses were tied. Abu Sabah was the old man and he was extremely respected by all the people, and especially by my father, who insisted on preparing his dinner.

The old man who the day before had judged the black mare to be promising turned to my father's side, and I saw a wave of pleasure come over his face. Before he could say anything, Abu Sabah pushed his hand under his clothes and got out a green piece of velvet tied to a small stick and said, 'The honour was not lost but given from the mother to her daughter—from the old to the young!' He gave the *qena* to my father. Now the old men smiled. Indeed, all the men smiled, and I, I think, along with them, though I was but a slip of a boy.

# CHAPTER 4

---

# *The Coming and the Going*

EVERYTHING went as usual that morning, except certain preparations in the *Shik*. It was late in summer. The sun became hot as soon as it rose and it was better to sit in the shade at the back of the tents.

The *Shik* was well swept, sprayed with water to settle the dust that might blow and to lessen the heat. Some new carpets were brought out, and many wool-stuffed leaning-bags were heaped in one corner of the big tent. The hearth was removed to a far corner. Tea and coffee pots were more than usual.

The same preparations were made in Nassralla's tent. The women and children in Nassralla's bigger tent moved to the small one. Then the tent was soon furnished to serve as a *Shik*, though two or three men were still there, making the hearth and putting the final touches to the things required in this second *Shik*. Haj Ibrahim, my grandfather, was active as ever, distributing his orders among the young men in the *Shik*: one had to spray water, a second had to tighten the ropes of the tent, and a third to prepare extra coffee cups and tea cups. Shehdi, his grandson, was sent up the hill to look out and see whether the men were coming.

I noticed that most of the men, especially the old ones, did not go to their daily work as usual, but stayed in the tribe. Even the small schoolboys, who were on holiday, came earlier than usual from the vineyards, driving their donkeys laden with baskets full of ripe grapes and figs. I saw some men of the other nearby tribes who came in great numbers, more than usual. Nothing was said

35

about their dinner, but food was directly brought for their horses.

It was clear that some people—strangers and important— would come that day. Why were they coming? Why was the other *Shik* being prepared? Why had the great number of foreign men come?

These questions seduced me, and diverted me from enjoying that holiday by going to Wadi Al-Hisi and joining my school-mates swimming in the natural pools. I stayed like the old, important people to see what was going to take place.

'It's a judging case,' my mother told me when I asked her. My grandfather, Haj Ibrahim, was one of the three recognized tribal judges in the Jubarat tribes, and I had seen him solving many intricate, dangerous problems. But I had never seen such prepar-ations made before. The case must be very important, otherwise there was no necessity for these preparations and making two *Shiks*. I wanted to know something about the case, but, as boys, we were not to interfere in things which were for men only.

The fire was set up and Hamad began to roast the green coffee beans on the glowing fire. He was talking to someone else who was sitting in front of him on the other side of the hearth. The other man was preparing the *mihbash* as the next step, the second instrument, to be used in the coffee-making. I was interested in watching how the green beans lost their colour gradually with the effect of fire, and the flat-ended bar moving them from one side to another, then Hamad moving the pan up and down to blow away the very thin—now yellow—layer which was separated from the beans by the heat. At this point some of the beans usually sprang out of the shallow pan, to be taken by a small child sitting close to the place. That day I was the child who followed the springing beans.

I had more than once seen the coffee put into the *mihbash*, but that day I asked Hamad if I could myself do the job. Hamad laughed, looked all round to see whether Haj Ibrahim was looking at us or not, and whispered, 'Give him the *mihbash*, Salem. Put your hands open like a cup on the opening of the *mihbash*.'

I did as he said and, as he turned out the roasted beans into my hands, I shouted, for I was being burnt by the very hot beans—

and some of them missed the opening and fell on the ground. Hamad was saved from comments when somebody said, 'Shehdi is signalling to us! They are coming.'

Haj Ibrahim began to allot the orders. 'Taleb, go and meet the men! Nassralla, you must go to your tent and see that everything is all right. You must stay there, because the other people will be coming very soon.'

Few minutes had passed after Nassralla and some other people had left, when many horses' heads appeared over the top of the hill where Shehdi was standing. There were about twelve horsemen coming towards the *Shik* in a group. Their horses were of different colours, while they themselves seemed, as they came near, to be of different ages. Twenty yards before reaching the *Shik* they were met by our people, and the *Shik* became empty except for the early-morning guests, who were all looking out at the newcomers. I stood with other children behind the women's part of the tent, holding to the long guy-ropes.

Haj Ibrahim was among the people who went outside, followed by his son Taleb. Each man of our people went to a horseman and caught his rein, but not one of them dismounted until the old white-bearded man, met by Haj Ibrahim himself, dismounted. He shook hands with Haj Ibrahim, while his horse was taken by Taleb to be tied.

The other horses were tethered, too. The guests entered the tents, welcomed by Haj Ibrahim and some other old men, while the young people were still outside and were on the point of quarrelling over the horses' nosebags. Everyone was trying to take more nosebags than the others. My father took one and called me to fill it with barley from our tent. I went there and returned with the full bag, which my father took and hung on the head of one of the better horses. In a few minutes, and before the men drank their coffee, the bags full of barley were hanging at the heads of all of their horses.

The old man with the white beard sat in the middle, near the partition between the men's and women's parts of the tent. His men sat on each side of him. He was leaning with his left elbow on a small heap of pillows. The guests first-arrived sat on both sides, the eastern and the western sides. The coffee was drunk and there was some talk, but nothing was said about the thing they had come for.

Half an hour later, another group of horsemen came from the east. Some of our men went to meet them as they followed Shehdi to Nassralla's tent. They were about the same number as the group in the main *Shik*. The same procedure was followed for the new group.

Tired by now of the old guests, I ran with the other children to see the latest comers. This time some of us, the older ones, took part in the welcoming procedure. I in my turn took one of the nosebags, not from a horseman, but from my cousin who had taken two. My mother was very pleased when she learnt that I had dealt with the bag myself.

Feeling that the most important things would be taking place in the main *Shik*, we all left for there, except for a few boys who were kept behind to serve as messengers. There in the main *Shik* I swiftly converted the *mihbash* into a small wooden stool by over-turning it, so as to be able to sit on it and see what was taking place. Some of the children sat near me, a few sat close-up to their fathers, pressing and peering, while the others stood in a group at the back of the tent. We were not sent away, because the *Shik* with men meeting was considered a practical school for the young boys as well as old men.

Nassralla, with some of the men who had come early in the morning, began to walk between the two tents, carrying the ideas of the one party to the other. They were trying to find the basis upon which the two parties could meet in one tent. It was about a murder, and so it was necessary to be sure of what would happen when the two sides met.

At last the negotiations succeeded and the two parties sat together in the original *Shik*. Bin Rashid's group, who had come first, sat in the southern part of the tent, while the Thwahta group sat on the northern side. The men of our tribe and the other guests sat in two lines, to the east and the west. Haj Ibrahim sat in the middle of the eastern line.

For a while there was complete silence. All the eyes were fixed on Haj Ibrahim. He said, 'Good evening, our guests. You know the customs.' Then, turning his face towards the left, he continued, 'Who is your guarantor, Bin Rashid?'

The old man with the white beard looked at the men on both sides as if he were looking for the man to guarantee him. 'Bin Rafie is the man,' he said.

All the people looked towards Bin Rafie, who was sitting opposite to Haj Ibrahim. The man was silent, and looked down as he heard his name. He must have been expecting that one of the disputing parties would nominate him as a guarantor, because without any hesitation he accepted. 'I am ready to stand for Bin Rashid, whatever may be the result,' Bin Rafie said.

Haj Ibrahim turned to the Thwahta group and said, 'Have you any objection, Thwahta?'

A middle-aged man of the Thwahta glanced quickly at his group before he answered, 'No, I haven't. He's trustworthy.'

Then the middle-aged man named his own guarantor, who, too, was accepted without any objection from the other side. Then the pledge was offered. The Thwahta offered one hundred pounds, so Bin Rashid was obliged to pay the same amount. The pledges were put on the carpet in front of Haj Ibrahim. It was well understood that the loser would lose his pledge and it would be taken by the judge as fee, while the pledge of the winner would be returned to him.

'Now,' Haj Ibrahim said, 'let us hear your case, Bin Rashid, since it was you who came first.'

All the faces turned to Bin Rashid's side, as he began to state his case in a low voice which could hardly be heard by the men at the end of the tent. He spoke the same introductory phrases, which were no more than greetings to the judge. Then he began to tell the details of his case.

'My nephew, the son of this man,' (and he pointed to the third man on his left), 'went one day as usual to look after his cows. He was young, twenty years old. He left the tribe as happy as any one of these young men near the fire. All this summer we have been preparing for his marriage.'

The old man paused for a while, then went on with his speech. 'At noon he went to water his cows on the lower part of Wadi Al-Hisi. There were many boys and girls doing the same. They were not of our tribe only, but also of the Thwahta and some other tribes. He was raising the water from the small well which contains better water than that in the small stream. Not far from him, under the tree, there was a group of boys and girls. He had been sitting with them before he left to get water for his animals. Then he was called by Khaleel, one of the Thwahta tribe.'

The boy's father was thinking deeply, with downcast head, as if he were reading something in the intricate, winding lines of the carpet in front of him. All the people there were completely silent, following the words spoken by the white-bearded old man and reading the expressions on the face of the boy's father.

'He had hardly turned his face towards the tree, when the sound of a shot was heard and Fahad fell into the well. The boys sped to the place and they found Fahad motionless in the red water. They got him out, but he had already died.'

The voice paused, on the brink of a moment, it seemed. One of the Thwahta group tried to comment, but the middle-aged man silenced him before Haj Ibrahim could do that.

'Khaleel was turned to stone,' Bin Rashid went on, 'and stayed under the tree. An old man of the Thwahta tribe announced that the boy was in Abu Jaber's face, and so no harm was done to him.'

Before he said this I had expected that something would happen to Khaleel as a kind of prompt revenge, but after I heard it I realized that nothing would happen. Now that it had been said he was 'in a sheikh's face,' no one of course would harm him : any harm done would strike at the sheikh himself. As children in our games we had done this more than once, and used to respect the rules. We often used it to involve neutral, peaceable boys in our quarrels. Sometimes this brought further fighting, sometimes the newcomer was involved only to clear up the dispute.

'Then in the night,' said Bin Rashid, 'and as we finished the burial service, two men came and asked a truce for two weeks. We could not refuse, because we are not of those who break the tribal laws. Before the two peaceful weeks passed, the same men came and asked us to nominate three judges to consider our case. So we did. It was the Thwahta turn to reject one of these three possible judges. Then we, too, had to reject one. The one left was you.' All the eyes turned to Haj Ibrahim.

'We are quite sure that you are the best to look into the case. I hope that, since we have come to your tent, we will have our rights in full, as it should be.'

Haj Ibrahim was silent all this time. He, as was his habit, was marking the sand with the stem of his long pipe. He stopped marking the sand, and turned to the middle-aged man and said, 'What have you to say, Bin Thabet?'

The midde-aged man began speaking fluently, as if he had learnt the words by heart. 'I don't want to add anything to what Bin Rashid has said, except about what took place under the tree before the accident happened. The gun was not Khaleel's gun : it was another's. It was the gun of Mohammad, one of our tribe. Khaleel, before shooting, asked him whether the gun was loaded, and Mohammad, who was occupied in a game with other fellows, said, "No." Thinking that it was empty, he wanted to have fun with Fahad, who was his close friend, but it was in God's hands and suddenly the misfortune happened. It was done by mistake and not intended at all.'

He turned towards Haj Ibrahim and added, 'You perhaps asked some of your boys who were there, and they must have told you that what I say is true and that Fahad and Khaleel were friends. We have come here ready to accept your sentence.'

The eyes of all the people again moved to Haj Ibrahim, whose turn then it was to speak. He began to retell Bin Rashid's account, adding some remarks, enquiries and explanations. He repeated nearly all that Bin Rashid had said, even the same words sometimes. That was the custom : the judge had to repeat the two parties' speeches, perhaps to make clear the vague points or to show that he had a complete conception of all the circumstances. Then he did the same for the Thwahta case. When he finished his speech about the case, he said, 'Now it is your turn, to make your negotiations.'

Men began to go outside the tent, to sit a few yards away and discuss the matter. The neutral men now held a small meeting with the Thwahta, then with Bin Rashid. Step by step Haj Ibrahim was informed of the results of their efforts.

At this interval some of us were called to bring water. I was asked, too. I took the opportunity to pass slowly by the men who were discussing near the tent. I tried to catch some of their words. I heard some of them, but I could not make anything of them. When I returned, I passed by the women's part of the *Shik* and found that it was full of women who were sitting silent, following

41

all stages of the trial. At the other side of the tent there were a few women preparing the guest's dinner. When I had brought the water, I sat with the other children, waiting for the last word to be said by the judge.

It was the time for dinner, and this was ready. But it had to be delayed till the sentence was heard. Haj Ibrahim again was ready so speak when all the men sat in their places.

'Now,' Haj Ibrahim said, 'it is clearly the case that the two parties are ready for reconciliation. Bin Rashid insists that he must hear the sentence, and then, if the judgment has been in his favour, he is free whether to forgive or not. It is said—and said truly—that right does not satisfy the two parties. I have no choice but to say what I know.

'In a case like yours it is very difficult to pronounce. Your boys were friends, but one of them killed the other. In our tribal law three things are not to be borrowed or given to others—women, horses and arms. We know, too, that arms are not to be played with. You see how difficult it is to judge. But I have to say the sentence.

'Out of my knowledge, which is built on our inherited traditions, I declare that the killing was done without any previous determination—nevertheless, the lives of people are not to be left for irresponsible men to play with. Bin Rashid has the right to ask what he likes, within our law, for the life of his son. He has the right to ask, and Bin Mishrif must pay.'

Bin Mishrif showed his readiness to fulfil his obligations, and the Thwahta too. 'Let Bin Rashid ask his right,' the middle-aged man said. 'We are ready to pay him his due. Here is Khaleel ready for punishment.'

He had barely ended these words, when a young boy came from Nassralla's tent, led by another man's hand and brought in the middle of a group. I did not then know who that young man was, but I learnt afterwards that he had, throughout the hearing, stayed with another man in Nassralla's tent. I followed the young man with my eyes, and saw him walk steadily up through the people to kneel in front of the father of Fahad. He did not then move.

The old man seemed puzzled at first, perhaps taken aback. I could not help standing up, as did the other children, to see what the father might do to the person who had killed his son. I noticed the curtain between the men's and women's parts moving, and I guessed that the women inside were trying to witness this critical moment. All the men in the tent were silent, too, looking from the young man to the old.

The old man continued to look at the young boy kneeling in front of him. Then he said, 'Neither money nor punishment can return Fahad to life—to marry and get children. Now he is in need of God's mercy. You killed Fahad, and for the sake of Fahad I set you free. Get up, my boy, and go. You are free.'

He said these words and took the boy by the hand. The boy was weeping when he got up.

All the Thwahta group went to the old man. They kissed his head, and shook hands with the other men.

The dinner was brought and all the men sat around the large plates full of rice and meat. Before the eating began, Haj Ibrahim said, 'In the name of our tribe I thank Bin Rashid for his generosity. I in my turn will return both the pledges, because your reconciliation in my tent is better than all money.'

I remember about thirty horsemen disappearing beyond the hill, those twenty-odd years ago. A horseman with a piece of white cloth in his hand was the first one to disappear over that sun-baked brow.

# CHAPTER 5

## *Once*

IT was just a day. It was one of those days when nothing particular happened.

I got up at dawn, like most of those among whom I was living—the people of our tribe. It was early in the summer, the time of early reaping. Many people had begun the harvest about two weeks before. Lentils and barley had to be reaped before wheat, because they ripened before the latter. These two kinds of plants lose much of their fruit if they are left for a long time after ripening. Thus it was their turn.

At that time of the year many agricultural labourers used to come in from the surrounding villages. In course of time they grew acquainted with the people and established a kind of friendship with our tribe. Some of these labourers brought their wives with them, though most of these women did not work, except to help in light tasks like preparing food or water. Occasionally they helped in collecting the reapers' small heaps and putting them on the stack. In spite of doing no hard job they were paid as much as their husbands.

All the people awoke. The *mihbash* was heard and I saw my father making his way to the *Shik*, to have the usual cup of coffee before leaving for Ghorab, our piece of land which we had begun reaping three days before. Most of the men used to go to the *Shik*, but not to sit for more than a few minutes. They just drank the morning coffee and then left, so the coffee used to be made earlier than usual. Haj Ibrahim used to get up particularly early, to start the fire and to begin preparing the coffee. Some men would get up and come to help him. He used not to go off as early as the other men, for he had to stay in the *Shik* in case a guest might come, when he should be there to receive him. But sometimes he left the tents and followed the people reaping in their fields. I had not myself seen him reaping, but certainly he had reaped when he was as young as his grandson, Shehdi, who now was driving his cart pulled by two mules and leaving the tribe. I wished that Shehdi had been going towards Ghorab, then I would have ridden with him as I had done many times before. But this time I had to go on foot.

Children were not asked to do any hard work, but sometimes they were told to work as messengers, to bring water for a thirsty harvester, to fetch a sickle for someone, or to drive the animals away from unreaped corn or the scattered heaps. When the children had nothing to do, they used to take their places among the reapers and imitate them in their work, but usually they were forbidden to do so because they left many uncut plants behind them. So, for the various reasons, children used to go with the other people when they were free from reading.

It was early in the summer, a few days after the beginning of our summer vacation as small boys at the tribe's elementary school, when I followed the group of people along the Sultani road. Some of the people were on foot, while others were riding animals—donkeys, camels and horses. There was some shouting : a man was calling his son to fetch something they had forgotten to bring with them, a shepherd was asking his friend where he would go that day, or a small child was trying to follow his parents while an old woman, perhaps the grandmother, was trying to restrain him.

I remember one of those children : he was Salmaan, a four-year-old. Nassra, his grandmother, could not persuade him with her sweet words. He stopped crying, and when she released him he ran quickly and nearly disappeared in the leaving crowd. Nassra stood in her place, laughing, and did not try to follow him. Perhaps she enjoyed the trick played by her small grandson. She did not wait long, before she returned to the tents.

I felt happy then, because I was not small like Salmaan, to be kept at home. But still I felt that I was unable to do what I wanted. I wanted to go with my grandfather's reapers, because I would be more free. My brother Ibrahim would make me and my brother Hassan work as true messengers. He used to say to us, 'In the field you must forget that you are schoolboys. You have to work.'

My father was more lenient. But most of the times he was away from the tribe, because he had been chosen by the government to work as a tax-collector. He accepted this job on condition that he worked in the same area—among Jubarat tribes—and this condition was agreed to. So he used to go away for three or four days and then return home for a night or two. Thus Ibrahim, as the eldest son, carried the responsibility of our father, sometimes helped by my uncles. He, in his position, had not the emotions that a father had. We felt, as children, that he treated us harshly. I think that we felt so because we compared his treatment with that of our father, who used to come more or less as a guest. Now I feel that Ibrahim was really a good-hearted man, but driven by the idea that he was less educated than others.

I found it a good opportunity that day to ask my father to let me go to my grandfather's field. I waited till he came out of the *Shik*, mounted his black horse and came along the Sultani road. As he came near me he said, 'What are you waiting for? Come! Give me your hand to ride pillion.' He stopped the horse, but I did not give him my hand.

'I want to go to my grandfather's field,' I said.

He laughed as he leant, trying to catch me by the hand, and said, 'Give me your hand and I'll drop you at the cross-roads.'

I rode behind him. Along the road he began to ask me some mathematical questions : I answered most of them. Then he asked me to recite the lines of verse that he had taught me and Hassan, and which later he taught to all my younger brothers :

> *Knowledge raises tents without poles,*
> *While ignorance destroys high palaces.*
> *The written word stays many years after*
> *The writer, who will decay underground.*

Then he began to recite to me *Alia and Issam,* a long love poem about a bedouin girl whose lover happened to kill her father. He promised to write it down for me, and I promised to learn it by heart.

We reached the cross-roads, and before he stopped his horse I jumped down and went along the road leading to Zinad, one of my grandfather's pieces of land. Its soil was a mixture of sand and clay: wheat was the best crop which it produced. Along the road I could see the cart tracks. I followed the track of one wheel which was still fresh, undamaged except by my footsteps and in some places by the traces of the blue pigeons, with their red legs and beaks, which came up early just as the sun rose. I knew that they would not stay for a long time, because they would leave very soon to drink from Wadi Al-Hisi after having had their breakfast. I knew their times of eating and drinking, because I used to go with my father to shoot them. They did not fly except when I came close to them.

Near the road I could see some of our people reaping. They were Abu Tamaa's family. Behind them, in the stubble, I could see also a flock of sheep and some cows. They were reaping lentils: I could distinguish the yellow-brown plants stretching in front of them.

I passed them and came to Om Al-Noor, a piece of land among three hills where there was a big thorny tree. Its name indicated that it was the place of light. As children we had been told that a light used to haunt that spot. I had seen it more than once, but I was not sure whether it was the light sent out by glowworms or fireflies, or if it was a light caused by a ghost which would not depart from that place. Twice in my life our tribe had spent spring there. I had not feared the light because the people were everywhere. But once they had left the place I was afraid to go there, especially at night.

I could still remember how one night we were walking along the road not far from the tree with my uncle—I, my brother Hassan and two other children—when he challenged us about who could put a mark of three stones under the tree. The only one of us to accept the dare was Hassan, who was a little older: he went there and in the morning we found the mark undisturbed. Now I passed by the tree, which stood calm and green in the yellow barley field at the foot of one of the hills. I felt that I could go there, but I was not sure whether that feeling would not leave me at night.

I came to a winding part of the road, where I saw how the

wheels of Shehdi's cart had gone a little away from the road as he negotiated one of these curves. On occasions, some cars passed along the Sultani road, and this part was the most difficult one. Not far from these curves were the houses of the Ziadeen, some families of our tribe. Near them I could see the huge heaps of newly reaped corn. It was not the time of threshing: it was still early.

As I drew closer to the houses I saw a man leading his camel, which hardly appeared under the enormous load. Reaching one of these giant stacks, he turned to the camel and shook the halter-rope, and soon the camel knelt on his foreknees, then settled. His owner began to untie the ropes binding the corn. Then I heard his shout before the camel arose, leaving the heavy load to be a part of the huge heap. Before I reached Zinad the man passed by me, riding on his camel. He was singing. I could not distinguish all the words of his song, but I still remember how the tune was moving up and down in accordance with the movements of the trotting camel.

On both sides of the road there were fields. Most of them were ripe, while a few were still green because they had been sown later. They appeared as small green squares among the broad, yellow fields, but I could still see some green winding lines spread over these yellow areas. They had been the beds of the small rivulets made by rain. As children we liked those green parts, because we could cut the wheatears there, roast them in the fire, blow away their husks, then eat the pleasant-tasting, roasted grain. We did that often, and we enjoyed it most on Thursdays in the afternoon, when we used to leave school earlier than usual.

Far away in one of the green parts I could see a cow grazing. It was on one of the slopes. Every now and then it raised its head, looked left and right, then returned to its eating. Perhaps it knew that it was doing a forbidden thing. Anyway, the poor cow did not enjoy its thieving for long, because before I went off behind one of the curves I saw a person, breast-high in the corn, running and driving the cow away quickly.

When I came up one of the hills I saw Zinad. There were many people and many animals, too. From a far distance there was a kind of confusion. I could not distinguish the varieties of the animals. Camels were mixed with cows, and cows with sheep.

But, the closer I came, the clearer I saw the animals and the people. Zinad was a big field to the left of the Sultani road. It had the greatest number of harvesters in the surrounding area. It stretched over a wide plain and covered two hills which were in its eastern part. The people now were in the part near the road. The reaping had begun few days before, and still the reapers were not far from the road. They were still far from the hills.

As I came nearer I could see the long line of reapers and I could hear their singing coming above the other noise made by the crowd of people and animals. They were singing enthusiastically. Behind them there were the cow-herds and shepherds moving in front of their beasts to keep them away from the heaps of corn or the unreaped parts.

I reached there, and soon I was part of that great crowd. I had nothing to do, so I went here and there. I saw now that the sheep were apart and also the cows. In front of the sheep I saw Salem, my grandfather's shepherd. He was leaning on his stick in front of his animals. Sometimes he raised himself and threw a small stone in front of a sheep trying to go through the small heaps behind the harvesters. He was mostly annoyed by the lambs, which were not as calm as their mothers. There were two other shepherds not far from Salem. They were more active than Salem. Both of them were moving lightly in front of their animals.

Shehadi, my cousin, was also standing in front of his cows. He was playing on his pipe. But his playing was out of place, because it was overcome by the reapers' loud singing. His cows seemed to be satisfied, for some of them were lying on the newly cut stalks. I came near him and he had to stop playing to return my greeting. He stuck his pipe under his belt because, I think, he himself felt it was not a suitable moment for playing.

Near the biggest heap there were the two mules eating from a small heap put for them. Shehdi, with two others, was loading the cart. They took armfuls of corn and put them in the cart. I ran to help them, not for the sake of help, but hoping that Shehdi would let me go with him and sit on the top of the corn. When we finished the work he told me that he was in a hurry and could not let me go with him and promised to take me the next time. Then he took his place on the cart and shouted 'dee' and the animals moved heavily under their weighty load. But as they went further they went faster. I kept on looking at them till they disappeared behind one of the curves. I knew that they would reappear, but I did not stay to see them, because I left for the reapers.

I passed among the small heaps. There were some women collecting these and carrying them to the stack. Thahab, a young village girl, was with them. She was the sister of Matar, one of the reapers. She could easily be distinguished, not only by her face, but also by her fair skin and green eyes. As I saw her I remembered what my grandmother used to tell us about a man called Jomaa, who was fond of having fun with the girls, especially the villagers.

Unfortunately Jomaa was short-sighted. One day Ali Abu Salamah, one of the most pleasant men in the tribe, brought a jar, put it near the cornstack and covered it with a piece of cloth like that which the girls put on their heads. He adjusted the draped jar to make it seem as if it were a sitting girl. When Jomaa came riding his horse he saw the supposed girl and passed by her more than once. Each time he got nearer. Ali, with the rest of the group, was looking on from a distance. At last Jomaa came close to the girl, perhaps said something to her and got no reply. At last he discovered the trick and broke the jar with a stick in his hand, while the witnesses ran at him, laughing loudly.

I thought, when I saw Thahab, that Jomaa was not to be blamed. Perhaps he had imagined the jar to be a very beautiful girl like Thahab.

Then I left the women collecting the sheaves and went to the reapers, who were busy in their work. I saw Taleb, my uncle, who was the last one on the right. I knew that the cleverest reaper should be in that part where the corn was still standing. He was working as a guide for the whole line of reapers. He could widen or shorten the cut. He also had to keep the line straight. He also led the singing.

When I was there he was singing, while the others repeated after him :

> *Fear not, our master,*
> *There'll be no reaping unless it is clean.*
> *Our master, it's time for our leaving.*
> *'I swore not to let you depart*

*Until your shadows increased.'*
*Our shadows have increased and gone so far away*
*The camels can lie on them.*

I ran and took a place near the reaper who was on the left and began to repeat the song with them. If I had known the fatigue that reapers met, then I would have realized what these words must have meant to old Hammad who was near me. Every now and then the man who was near Hammad helped him by reaping a part of the crop in front of the old man. I saw that some men were competing, each one trying to surpass the other. I myself tried to compete with Hammad, so I took a very small line and began to cut the plants. I overtook Hammad, who had not changed the routine of his work. But, as I looked backward, I saw that Hammad was re-reaping the part that I had reaped.

I noticed that the rhythm of the songs increased in pace and that the sounds became louder. Then I saw Hammad turning his face towards the north: he smiled, then went on again. I, too, turned to the north and saw my grandfather riding on his chest-nut mare. The reapers had felt his coming and begun to work harder. The women began to collect more quickly, too. I knew that they did not fear him, but, as I think now, they respected him and were encouraged by his coming. As he reached the small heaps he greeted the harvesters in a loud voice, and they answered in a loud voice, too:

*Fear not, our master,*
*There'll be no reaping unless it is clean.*

I saw him getting down from his horse, tying the halter-rope to the front of the saddle. He slapped the mare on her neck and she went to the unreaped part of the field. I knew that no one would drive her away, because the well-known horses had to be respected as their owners. Haj Ibrahim walked behind the reapers and passed by me also.

'The schoolboys are good reapers today,' he said. 'How do you find harvesting, boy?'

'Better than school, grandfather,' I answered. At that time I really felt that anything was better than going to school and staying for about eight hours, taught by one teacher.

Hammad, my neighbour, hearing my answer, turned towards me, shook his head, and smiled. My grandfather seemed unconvinced, too, because he said, 'Ask Hammad which is better.' Then he left, going round the unreaped part : he did not go into it as his horse had done.

Soon the cart came, and when I saw it I left my place near Hammad and ran to meet Shehdi. While it was on the road the cart went quickly, but, as it came to the reaped part, it went slowly so as to avoid the scattering animals. So I was able to climb in and not to get down till the cart reached the big stack.

Near the stack there was a camel, being loaded by three men. They soon finished their work, fixed the net with its ropes and hooks. Then the camel rose. Led by a man it left the place. Then it was the cart's turn to be loaded. Soon it was loaded and left with me on the top of the corn.

Shehdi tried to get me to sit near him, but I insisted on staying in my place. So he began to drive slower than before. When we reached the threshing floor we got down. Taking a fork, he began to fling the corn down. I tried to help him, but I could not.

When we finished, he drove towards the tents to fetch the food for the harvesters. The tents were silent, except for a few cock-crows. The cart stopped in front of my grandfather's tent. There was no one in the *Shik,* apart from two dogs lying asleep in the righthand corner. In the women's part my grandmother was shaking the milk in its goatskin bag. It seemed as if she were at the end of her job, because soon she stopped shaking. Then, after getting the butter out, she gestured to Shehdi to take the food. Then she put the milk-bag in the cart. I did not go to our tent, for fear that my mother would make me carry the food for the reapers. After having drunk water, we left the tents.

When we arrived we found that all the reapers and the women were sitting near the big stack. In the middle there was my grandfather, leaning against the piled corn. Soon the food was brought down from the cart. The people divided into two parts, women in one and men in the other. The shepherds and cow-herds nearby were invited, a few accepting and the others excusing themselves.

The meal soon finished, but men sat on talking and smoking, while women sat not far from them, chatting in low tones. I went to the women's circle, because I liked to hear my aunt's pleasant talk.

Half an hour after the meal, the work began again. It became harder as the sun grew hotter. The shepherds and cow-herds began to leave for Wadi Al-Hisi to water their animals. After a while the animals were in one long line going northwards to the Wadi.

It was about two o'clock when it was the time for leaving. The reapers left before the shepherds and cow-herds returned. As we were leaving for home and before we went far, I saw the groups of blue pigeons hovering over our heads, then coming down in the newly reaped area, the place which we had just left.

Yes, it was just one of those days of my boyhood when nothing in particular happened. It was one of those golden links in the golden chain which bound me to my people, and us to our land, and us all to our way of living.

The chain now is stretched. Its links have been passed rapidly through many fingers, much as we pass our beads up and down, round and about, as we sit and finger, or count out our luck, or from time to time put up a prayer. My chain has been stretched, wrung in the many hands of men, slipped through the fingers of God. It is no longer the shining, fresh gold which I knew as a boy.

But it still is my treasure, and today my solace. And perhaps it still is my and our hope.

# CHAPTER 6

# *Little Birds*

'I wish that I had a daughter,' my mother often says. 'Then she would help me. Girls are kinder than boys.'

I have heard these words uttered by my mother on different occasions, but especially when she has a lot of work to be done. The words are most sincere when she sits near the big tub, washing the family clothes. Her face becomes red and the sweat runs down her cheeks, to mix with the clothes-washing water.

I can always picture her washing the clothes, then walking slowly to hang them—at first, on the tent ropes, later on the ropes between the tree and a ring fixed in the outside wall. She used to walk slowly, and sometimes stop for a moment's rest before reaching the rope. It did not come to my mind to help my poor mother until I went far from her and personally felt the great troubles she had and the truth of her words.

Before I went out from the home, the words were just an ordinary complaint to which I did not pay attention : but now, to me, they are more than the words of a normal grumble. More than once I have tried to wash with her, but she always refuses.

I do not forget how one Friday she got up early in the morning, prepared our breakfast, then went under the big, thick tree with the hanging branches and began her ordinary job—to wash our clothes. I felt that she was in need of help, because she had been complaining of a severe headache for the past two days.

'Shall I help you, mother?'

She smiled, as she was wringing one of my brother's shirts with her hands, and said, 'You are a man and this job does not suit men—and anyway you can't do it. If Abla were here, she would help me. But I have to work till I see you married. Perhaps your wife will help me.'

I tried to convince her that I could do the work, and told her how I did it all by myself for a full year. But she refused, and showed her sadness for the trouble I had met near the washing basin.

Abla was not there to help my mother, and she will not come again ever. She was four years old when I saw her the last time. She had the same features as those of Yahia, my younger brother. She was beloved by both my father and mother because she was the only girl in the family. She was envied by her elder brother, but still she was beloved by all the family.

It was a Thursday when I left school as usual, accompanied by the group of boys. It was Thursday afternoon. The teacher had left for his village to see his children and to look after his family affairs. We used to be happy on Thursdays because they were followed by the week-ends. All the boys were happy, because they would spend a gay Friday away from the school and its troubles. We used not to bring our food with us that day, for we had to leave at eleven o'clock in the morning. In spite of being hungry we played along our way home, sometimes running and sometimes jumping.

In one of the gullies on our way there was a small tunnel, about four yards in length and hardly big enough to allow one boy to squeeze himself through it. It was made by erosion. Hamad was a thin boy who used to slide cleverly through that tunnel.

Four boys tried it that day: two succeeded and the others failed. Hassan was a fat boy. Challenged by Hamad, he threw himself in the hole and began to struggle, trying to get through. But he could not move, either forward or backward. He stuck in the middle and began to shout for help. Some of the boys stood around laughing, while others thought seriously of the problem.

'I'll slip in behind,' Hamad said, 'and take him by the legs—and then you'll drag me out.'

Without waiting for an answer, he entered the hole and caught hold of Hassan's feet. We began to drag Hamad out by his legs. In a few minutes Hassan was brought out, with dirty clothes and small grazes on his arms and right cheek. We all laughed, except Hassan, who was busy cleaning his clothes.

'I challenge you in swimming,' Hassan said to Hamad, who was now to one side, hopping up and down, unable to stop laughing. 'Tomorrow I'll wait for you at the pool in Wadi Al-Hissi.'

Hamad accepted the challenge, and we all agreed, except me, to meet at the pool the next day. We used to go there on Fridays and have a happy time swimming, playing, and sometimes hunting the small birds which used to come in great numbers.

At noon the shepherds and cow-herds would come with their animals for watering and to have two hours' rest. The animals knew the place where they were accustomed to drink, and they used to go there directly. In these two hours we would sit with the cow-herds and shepherds under the big trees scattered around the Wadi. Sometimes we shared their food—and used to find it better than ours, which we had either at school or at home. I liked very much the cheese they used to make themselves, especially that which was made by Shehadi, my cousin.

Some of these cow-herds and shepherds had been at school like us, and they frequently repeated that they wished they could return to being schoolboys. We could not believe them, because we felt that they were more free than us : they could go wherever they wanted, they could rest when they wished and, in addition, they had no heavy homework to be done. There was no teacher to punish them if they had not done their duties. I could not believe these shepherds, until I myself tried their life and realized the troubles they sometimes met.

As we wandered home, I told my friends that I was going out shooting the next day with my father. On his free days he used to take his double-barrelled shotgun (exactly as old as myself), then mount our black horse and go shooting, sometimes alone and sometimes accompanied by me or by one of my brothers. He used to go either to Wadi Al-Hisi, to shoot duck and other waterfowl, or to the gullies where there were coveys of red-legged partridges. His horse was trained to stop each time he saw a bird, and thus enabled his rider to shoot.

I was happy that time, because my father was going to Wadi Al-Hisi to shoot duck, though not in the same part where my schoolmates would be the next day. Perhaps, after swimming, they might come over to our side and help me in putting up the birds towards the place where my father would be kneeling in a small hide covered with a thorny green plant. And they would share with me in the birds: my father would give them some, as had occurred more than once.

It was at the end of spring: corn and grasses were about to dry and the young birds were flying behind their mothers. I used to hear the skylark singing up in the sky, but at that season it was singing not quite so high above us, and I liked it more and more. We passed by some empty nests, which we discovered when we were looking for various edible plants.

We came up the hill where we were able to see the tents. They were many, but two weeks later they would be separated in small groups for reaping and threshing time. Some of the cornfields were ripe, while others were about to ripen. A few mechanical implements were coming into use, but still the manual work prevailed. Everyone used to work in his own field and sometimes hire some of the neighbouring villagers to help him. But, should he be behind-hand, without any call for help all the neighbouring people would hasten to give a hand for one or two days, and this 'aid', as it was called, was appreciated by the man, who might kill a lamb for the helpers.

We all noticed that there was something extraordinary in the tribe. A lot of people were gathered in front of a tent, which we realized later was ours. Some of the people were entering and some coming out. We began to guess at the reason, and most of us thought it to be one of those roaming ᵖedlars, with brightly-coloured sweets among his stock-in-trade.

'But look!' Hamad said. 'There is neither a cart nor a donkey. There are only people there—men, women and children.'

'It must be something else,' the oldest boy said.

We all hurried towards the tents and went to our tent. There I saw a group of people, some sitting and others standing. I felt that some of them were looking at me. Before I could go in, I was called aside by Ali, one of the tribe's merry people. He began to talk with me about things I used to ask him to tell me about, but this time I felt that I was not in need of his speech. I left him quickly, in spite of being begged by him to stay, and entered the tent.

My mother was sitting near the bed of Abla, my sister. There were some women, my uncle, and some other small children who were trying to discover what was taking place by pushing themselves through the crowd. I pushed myself, too, and saw my mother laying her hand on Abla's forehead. The small girl was lying motionless. I knew that she had been feeling pain two days before, but it had not been serious.

My mother looked at me, but did not say anything. Abla's face was turned towards the south. I realized she was dying, and that the people outside were awaiting her death. There was no time to send her to a doctor, and thus she suffered her pains alone with my mother.

A few minutes later Abla died. No one wept, except my mother, my grandmother and me. My younger brother cried a little, too, but as a matter of manners, not knowing the meaning of death.

About an hour later the girl was prepared for burial. She was put in a new piece of white cloth. The religious ceremonies were done. Then my father put her in front of him on his black horse and went to the tribe's cemetery.

A few men, with the necessary tools, went before him to prepare the grave. My mother, with some other women, followed them. I followed them, too. My young brothers also tried to follow us, but they were forbidden to by my aunt, and she stayed with them at home.

We reached the cemetery, which was near the newly built houses. There were many graves scattered among the thick trees, which grew without any order. I had not visited that place, except on occasions of death.

Abla was laid in the grave and then covered by the sand. Two stones were fixed at the two ends of the grave. Then water was sprayed over it. My mother kept near the grave all the time, but she did not do or say anything, except that she kissed my small sister as she was lying in the bottom of her grave.

Then we all left, and Abla was left alone. I began to think of what our teacher used to say to us about what might happen after one's death. He told us that dead children would become the small birds in paradise. They had done no evil things to be punished for. Reaching that conclusion, I rested, and began to think of my sister as a small red-tailed bird in the green paradise, for I imagined it green through my teacher's lesson and from the old women's tales.

When we reached the tents, I found one of my younger brothers waiting for us away from the tents. He ran to meet my mother as soon as he saw her.

'Where is Abla?' he asked.

'She went far away.'

'Won't she come, mother?'

'No, she'll not,' said my mother sadly. 'She is dead.'

The small boy had no clear idea about death. He said, 'I'll go and ask my father to bring her.'

The next day was Friday. I neither went with my father out shooting, nor with my friends to swim in the Wadi Al-Hisi pools.

# CHAPTER 7

# *The Return*

UPON a hill and among many high trees there was a one-roomed house. That was the school of Al-Jubarat, our tribe which had fourteen sub-branches and lived on both banks of Wadi Al-Hisi. The hill on which was the school was in one of the *wadi's* curves. When one stood on the top of any of these hills, one could see the groups of tents: some were far and others near. They looked like dull black spots on a green painting. They were necessary to show the beauty of that picture.

The boys from far tribes used to come to that lonely school on horses or donkeys, while we used to cover the distance on foot because the school was on our land. Nevertheless we had to get up early, to drink some fresh milk, to put our simple food in the small cloth bags which contained our few books, and to leave the tents before sunrise.

We used to go to school as a group, so we had to call each other before leaving. We envied the shepherds when we passed them by, because we imagined that they were happy as they had not to go to school and to meet that strict old teacher. The happiest days for us were Thursdays, when he used to go to his family in the neighbouring village, or the days when we got an invitation for him. The lazy boys used to be punished by being made to get grass for his donkey. I knew many who intended to take that opportunity of getting out of school, because I had myself done that more than once.

One night, when many men were in the *Shik,* my father announced that the teacher would be our guest the next night. I could not sleep then for my excessive joy at that unexpected invitation, and I thought that many of the boys who had heard the pleasant news were doing the same. I got up earlier than on any day before and took my bag, but I found that I had forgotten to take my food and my mother had to come after me with it. That day we hurried to school.

I found the teacher on the eastern side of the school, dealing with the food of his white donkey under the biggest tree, always reserved for his beast. He smiled when he read the invitation, and told me to ring the big copper bell. Lessons passed quickly that day and few boys were punished. In the afternoon the teacher mounted his donkey and we followed him, envied by the boys from other tribes. As we were crossing the green fields, some of the shepherds came across to greet the teacher because he had taught them once. When we came near I ran quickly to announce the arrival of the teacher, but his donkey, having glimpsed the tribe's donkeys, forestalled me by a crescendo of braying. Men heard us and came quickly to meet the teacher, for it was the custom to meet the respected guest outside the tents and take his animal to be tied and fed. All the small boys stood near the tent: no one entered except me, and a few other boys who were called to recite some poems in the presence of our teacher and our fathers.

That night I heard my father talking about a grand school in Beer Al-Saba, the town where he used to go two or three times a year to discuss some of our tribal affairs with the government. 'It is a great school with red tiles and many trees around it,' my father said. 'Most of the boys there are sons of bedouin sheikhs. They wear the same dress as ours. They can learn many things.' Then he declared that he had decided to send me there.

The teacher agreed at once and praised the idea. Some of the men agreed, but others said that it was very difficult for such a small boy to be sent to a far town among cars and strange people. But my father convinced them of the wisdom of the new idea, and hoped that many would follow him and send their children to be doctors or engineers like Ali, the son of one of the bedouin sheikhs, who had become a very famous doctor.

The idea was not new to me, because my father used to tell me about that school when we were alone out hunting. He would tell me how he would be proud when I was the first among all other bedouin boys at the school. The new idea for me now was that I had to leave the tribe just at the end of that summer vacation.

It was in the evening at the end of that summer when the *Shik* was full of men. They sat as they usually did, but I was the matter of their speech. Some women came to our tent, so as to show their feelings to my mother or, perhaps, to see hers at the departure of her small child.

I went to the *Shik* to say goodbye to the men. I was obliged to stay there, while my small friends were standing in front of the crowded tent because they could not find room there. They waited for a long time, then left the place one by one. I heard them shouting while they were playing 'the wolf and the sheep', one of my favourite games. So I left the tent unseen by the men, who forgot me and the school and began to discuss their daily problems of weather, harvest and animals.

We played a good game that night, but it was interrupted more than once by a boy saying, 'Tomorrow, at night, who knows where you will be?' Our game ended when my father called me to sleep so as to get up early the next morning.

Next morning I rode behind my father on our dun horse and left the tents, accompanied by my cousin on his black, so as to bring back our horse after we reached the nearest bus-halt, which was about five miles from our tribe's place. Many people were at my farewell, because I was the first boy of the tribe who had to leave his parents for such a long time. I felt sad when my father spurred the horse, but I became sadder when I saw my mother waving to me with one hand and holding, with the other, one of my small brothers who was trying to follow us, thinking that we were going hunting. I could not stop my tears when for the last time I turned my face back, to see that some of the people were still standing near their tents while others had left their places and were returning to their usual life: I was accustomed to hearing that to look back on leaving was a bad habit, without getting an explanation, but at that moment I knew the reason. Our white dog followed us in spite of my cousin's threats. He did not leave us until we reached the halt.

In the evening we reached Beer Al-Saba. My father showed me

the school when we passed by, but I was unable to see anything except the red tiles which appeared among the high eucalyptus trees.

We spent that night in the town, and because I was tired I slept at once. When I got up in the morning I heard the great noise made by the car-horns and by sellers of vegetable and fruit, who were selling by auction. Everything was new and strange for me, except my father, who kept near me all the time and told me that soon I would enjoy the life of that beautiful town, as he called it.

After having our breakfast, we left for the school. We passed through a large gate with green iron bars. In the school yard I saw many boys in bedouin dress. They were very clean, and calmer than those in the school which I had left. As I was passing they gazed at me, perhaps hoping to know me. They gathered in groups as my father entered that old silent building followed by me.

Inside the school I saw many teachers, who were different from our teacher: they were young, bare-headed, and with smart suits. We were led to the headmaster's office. He was a grim, dark man with a red fez on his head, sitting at a big desk. His room was decorated with pictures of the school activities, and on a shelf behind him there were many golden and silver cups which, I read, had been won in games. After welcoming us, he called a certain teacher to show me my bed in the big hall, and my classroom, and to give me a key for my locker. When everything was done, he led me back to say goodbye to my father, with whom I went as far as the green barred gate, where he kissed me and reminded me to be polite and to work hard so as to raise the fame of our tribe. I stood at the green gate as he went without turning his face back. As he went out of sight the bell began ringing, so I ran to join the line of our class.

At noon we were called by a bell to our dinner. At dinner there was complete silence and strict order. I missed my small friends, the big green tree under which we used to have our dinner, the way in which we used to get our food from our small cloth bags, and how sometimes we invited another group sitting under another big green tree to have their dinner with us.

In the evening, after the lessons finished, all the boys except me, and two or three who were as new as me, began to play their games, of which I knew most—but I was unable to take part in any, because I was completely distraught. I went to the northern part of the playground and turned my face towards the north, because I wanted to smell the air that came from our hills. I imagined my father in his white clothes going back home and coming down the wide road where I used to meet him. He was indeed very sad when he went home, as my mother told me afterwards, to a degree that made her think something had happened to me, but he told her that the cause of his sadness was that he missed my meeting him as was usual when he came from a journey.

The sun began to sink, but not in the same way as it did in the country : it sank quickly as I became more sad. There were no hills to stand on and see the wide country with all its beauty, the sheep going home in long lines after their shepherds, who, playing their pipes, might be thinking of their sweethearts or of the place where they had to go the next morning. Then I remembered how I used to go home, my dog meeting me, my mother sitting beside the hearth preparing our supper, and my small brothers playing in the sand or on the heaps of the new-cut grass.

The loud sound of the bell broke these thoughts. I felt the boys running past me and taking their places in a long line for supper. I followed them, and took my place at the end of the line because I was the last to come.

All these bedouin boys might once have had their own thoughts shattered by that old bell as I had, because a week later I stopped thinking too much of my people and joined the boys in their games and entertainments. I played basket-ball, I went on walks to the town, to the British War Cemetery—I did all the new things.

Four months had passed slowly before we were allowed to leave the school for our families. There was great joy among us, and everyone began to pack his clothes waiting for that promised Thursday. On Wednesday evening we were allowed to go down to the town for shopping, so I bought some small toys and sweets for my brothers with the little money which I had saved for that purpose only. On Wednesday we did not sleep, and kept on singing and dancing all night. Our teachers enjoyed these songs and dances so much that they promised to give us the chance to repeat that party, once a month at least, the next term.

In the morning I went, without waiting for breakfast, to the station and got in the bus which had brought me with my father the first time. I was sure of the place where I had to get down, so I told the driver to drop me there. As I got down, the bus left. I saw the people turning their faces towards me, and I can still remember the old lady who waved to me. Then I was alone, looking at the green cornfields and the birds flying and singing happily. I went along the road among the young cornfields full of multi-coloured flowers. Here and there, both on the right and the left among the green fields, I could see some men and women collecting the weeds and gathering them in big heaps. I saw a man walking behind his camel, which was carrying a very great load of grass. I went after him quickly and, when I reached him, I asked him about the place of our tribe. He told me and offered his help, but I thanked him and went on alone.

When I came up on a hill, I saw many cows and sheep on a wide plain. They were on both sides of the road. I could see also the shepherds and cow-herds sitting together on a small knoll. I thought I recognized them by my grandfather's red horse and our white and black cow. My guess was right, because as I came near the boys looked at me, one shouted and some of them came to meet me. I was extremely happy to meet them and so were they to meet me. They told me about the place of the tribe, and Salim insisted on accompanying me to carry my bag. While we were walking, Salim gave a brief account of what had happened in the tribe after my departure. Sometimes he told me things which had taken place before my leaving.

'Ibrahim, your brother, married Fatmah. It was really a very good day, especially the horse race,' he said. 'Your black mare bore a very beautiful filly foal. No one died, all the people are well. I know a partridge nest with the small birds—I'll show it to you when you come out with us on one of the coming days.'

Salim went on giving his report till we came up a hill and I saw the tents on a wide, green and flowery plain. I felt such a great joy I even wanted to run to the tents.

'That's your tent, it's that one near your grandfather's big tent,' Salim said, pointing. We were coming from the eastern side, so we could see what was inside the tents. There were a few men in the *Shik,* and some small boys and girls playing in front of the tents. The goatskin milk-bags were hanging on the front poles. There were some women sitting at the southern part of one tent.

Seeing us, the dogs ran and barked, but when they came near they knew us and stopped. Having heard them, one man came out of the *Shik,* put his hand to his brow, and then turned towards the sitting men. Soon I saw a number of them come out, and the women gazing at me. It was certain they knew me, because my youngest brother ran towards me, shouting, then stopped for a while as if to take me in : and then he ran very quickly. As he reached me he hung his arms round my neck and began to kiss me while his eyes were shut. My mother, father and many other relations were in front of the tents. Before we reached them, my small brother told me lots of his tales.

It was a happy meeting. I could not sleep that night, though I greatly needed sleep. I found that everything was the same, but I enjoyed it more because of those months I had spent in the school. I felt free as one of those birds I had passed on my journey. Three weeks passed as if they were three days, and I went back to school at last with great sadness.

Two years had gone by when I came, for the last time, back from school. It was in the afternoon in the early summer when I got down from the bus at the usual spot. Everything was silent. The wheatfields, lentils and barley were yellow and ripe. Here and there I could see some newly reaped strips of land : they were clean, except for the big heaps of corn ready to be carried either on camels or in the new carts pulled by mules—not by horses, because it was shameful for a good man to let his horse pull a cart. I felt happy, because I thought that I would have the chance to get on these carts, either when they were full or empty.

I went on and on, but I could not see anything except some small birds and groups of blue pigeons quartering the reaped parts of the fields. They were picking up grain. Some of them were on the road, following the footprints of camels to find a better opportunity of getting more grain. They flew off when I came near, either to the neighbouring fields or further up the

66

road. I could see neither people nor animals. It was completely strange.

Then I remembered what I had heard when I was at school about the Israeli attack on one of the neighbouring villages and that many people were killed. The sun was going down and I wished that it would not, for I felt great loneliness. Even the pigeons began to leave the road. They flew up and disappeared behind the deserted hills to the west. I could not see anything speaking of life, except the marks left by the pigeons' feet on the sandy parts of the road. I began walking more quickly, so as to reach before sunset the place where our tribe stayed in summer time near our newly built houses.

When I came near I saw the houses—silent, like tombs. On the northern side, not far from them, there were white trodden spots in one of the harvested fields. On these spots there were small black stones, three on some and more on others. I knew them all—white trodden spots from newly removed black tents, and black stones of hearths recently deserted. At that scene I felt my heart sink. But I went to the place.

There was nothing but some old rags, ropes, pegs, broken pots, and the places for feeding animals. Not far from the biggest spot, which I guessed to be the place of my grandfather's tent, I saw a white bitch. She was my grandfather's. I was surprised, but it became clear to me when I saw her four small puppies. They all looked at me when I came near as if they found in me a new companion, or they might be thinking that the tribe was coming back. The mother did not bark, but moved her tail gently and came near me. I was sure that she knew me.

A feeling of extreme sadness came over me when I looked to the west and saw the sun's red rays going down behind the hills which had once been the place of an active, full and happy life. I decided to leave this place before darkness, so I went up to the houses where the granary was and the big tree under which we used to sit in the summer time.

I called the dog to follow me. She waited for a minute, looked at her small puppies, then followed me. She kept on looking back from time to time, and before I reached the tree she stopped, in spite of my continuous calling. When I saw that she would not follow me, I went on even sadder and more afraid.

I was alone when I reached the tree. No one was there but a flock of hundreds of small birds come to roost. They paid no attention to me when I approached, but went on with their chirruping. I looked everywhere, but I could see nothing except the white spots with black stones, and I could hardly see the sad dog sitting on her haunches with her face towards me. It was in vain that I called her. She did not move. She was silent as those small black stones.

I made up my mind to follow the wide road that led to the east and passed through Wadi Al-Hisi, thinking that it was the safest road. Before I had gone a few hundred yards I could hear the sad, mournful howling of my grandfather's dog. I felt as if she were calling me, but I went on with tears in my eyes.

I did not feel much thirst, except when I came near Al Wadi, where there was a small stream. As soon as I came near I became afraid, because we had been told, when we were small children, that many beasts used to visit that *wadi* for drinking at night. Despite my great fear I had no choice but to get through Al Wadi, so I opened a small knife I had in my pocket and went on. When I drew near I could hear the sound of frogs breaking the silence of night.

Then, in the middle of my drinking, I heard a voice call out, 'Who are you?' I was terrified and felt my hair bristling and said my name without thinking.

'Don't be afraid,' a familiar voice said, 'I am Ibrahim.' It was my elder brother, with three other men. He told me that they had come with their camels at night to get some of the corn that the tribe had been forced to leave.

As we went on together, they told me a lot of things, and I became less afraid but more sad. 'Let a few days pass and we shall be back,' Shehdi, my brother's regular companion, said.

Eighteen full years have passed and we are still prevented from going back. But usually in the evening, when I am alone, I can recall the white trodden spots with the small black stones and the white dog sitting on her haunches in the dusk. And then, when I am alone and lonely, I even imagine that I can hear the wailing, the weeping, in her voice.

# CHAPTER 8

---

# A Household a Little Way Off

A FEW miles from Wadi Al-Hisi, on the western side, there is a big *wadi* which becomes wider and wider as it goes winding towards the west till it reaches the Mediterranean. I do not know the place where it begins, but I know that it passes through the land of most of the Al-Jubarat tribes. It crosses our land. Many of the Diqses planted fruit trees in that valley. Except for these green parts, it was forlorn and lonely.

In one of its parts, and in a place where the gully leaves our land for Al-Sawarkah land, my father had chosen a spot for planting figs and vines. I did not remember when my father had done that, because I had seen those green trees as long as I could recall. They were a few hundred on both sides of the gully, which crossed a piece of land of ours about ten donum in area. It was good and productive soil. Thus a few trees were sufficient for our family and for the frequent gifts sent by my father to his friends who had none.

My father used to work all the year round in that valley, at the times when he was free from his other work. In spite of its being far from the place of our tribe, it became more and more visited by the members of our family. I used to go there in summer-time in the school's summer vacation, and then I went there nearly every day. There was neither a wall nor a hedge round it, so I used to go there in summer-time with Hassan, my elder brother, to keep it in order and sometimes to remove a stray beast.

In the upper part of the gully and near our orchard there was Abu Zaid's orchard. There was a line of prickly-pear, with some of the branches over our land and the others on Abu Zaid's side.

He had planted that line, but he was generous and asked us to use the fruit which was on our side. He had also three vines which used to ripen later than the other kinds, so he used to send us baskets of their grapes when the other vines had already finished He used to live there in his orchard in a mud house with a wood roof which was covered also with mud.

He was called Abu Zaid because of his dark colour, his well-built body and his silent nature, which were the same as the characteristics of Abu Zaid, one of the historic Arab heroes. It seemed to me that having that name had changed his nature. Living alone was an unusual thing among the bedouins, so Abu Zaid seemed to us a strange man. I myself used to feel a kind of fear when I passed along the *wadi* through his orchard. He had three cows, a camel and a black donkey, besides two savage dogs.

When I came to know Abu Zaid, his wife had already died and he was living with his two daughters and two boys. The elder daughter was about seventeen, but as long as I had known her she had been acting as mother for the other small children. Her maternal feeling went so far that it occupied every part of her heart. Her father dealt with her as if she were not his daughter but a friend, who, seeing him in trouble because of his small children, had come to help him by looking after them. Many times we asked him things and had him answer, 'Go and ask her.' Kathra was her name, but he scarcely mentioned that : it sufficed him to say 'she' or 'her'.

The father used to stay at home when he had no work outside. I had not seen anyone from his tribe come to visit him or to help him. I did not know any reason for that, except that he was a few miles far from them and might have been forgotten by them. He was better known by our tribe, and some children thought him to be one of the Diqses. But I had not seen him even once in our *Shik*.

I saw him sometimes speaking with my father, and I felt that they were friends more than mere neighbours. He used to insist upon my father drinking a cup of coffee, and my father was the only man with whom I had seen him share the coffee from his badly-burnt coffee pot. Through being busy my father, sometimes, refused to go over, but Abu Zaid used to come walking slowly in his white flowing clothes, carrying his black coffee pot and two cups, so my father was obliged to leave his work to the labourers and to sit not far from them, drinking coffee and gossiping with Abu Zaid.

In winter and spring time we used to go seldom to that orchard, just for ploughing the soil twice or thrice and pruning the vines. At such times Abu Zaid's family were left alone. I could not know how they felt when they became alone, but I think that they were accustomed to that kind of life. They were not completely cut off from people: they could see the school on a hill a few miles to the north-west and some of the mud houses on other neighbouring hills. Some people might pass by them, but they would not stop, because it was well-known that Abu Zaid was of those people who preferred to stay alone rather than to receive a man whom one had nothing to do with.

'Who is not good for you may be good for others.' That was my father's reply to many people who described Abu Zaid as a man of no use and no friends.

It was two summers before we were driven savagely from our country for it to be occupied by a foreign people, when I went with big-brother Hassan to look after the orchard. We were welcomed by our friends, Abu Zaid's sons, and by their sister, who was about twenty years old at that time. She asked us a lot of questions about Mariam, who was nearly of her age. She seeemed more beautiful than before. Sometimes she looked to the west, as if she were looking for something, but I did not notice anything extraordinary.

We kept on coming daily, because the fruit was ripe. In the evening we used to load four full baskets on our two donkeys and go back home. Kathra visited us more than usual that year. She was sitting with us one day, when a shepherd came, greeted us, and asked if we had some fruit to sell. Hassan told him, smiling, that we were not fruit-sellers, and asked me to bring him two or three bunches of grapes. The shepherd refused to take anything without paying, and left before I could bring him the grapes.

That shepherd also kept on coming near the gully and began spending most of the day there. He was not of our tribe, but he became familiar to us because of his frequent visits. We also became accustomed to the sound of his pipe, especially at evening when we prepared ourselves for going home. There were two strange things about that shepherd : he used to come alone and he never went near Abu Zaid's house or land.

Kathra began staying with us for some hours each day. Sometimes when we used to leave she did not go directly to their home, but walked slowly among the vines.

It happened that we had not gone one day to the orchard and next day came later than usual, in the afternoon. We sat under a very big fig tree under which we used to sit daily, and were about to leave that tree and start collecting the grapes, when Kathra came up the gully from the northern side. She seemed to be at once tired and excited. Her face was red, but she seemed to be happy, because she was smiling when she greeted us and passed towards their house. A few minutes later the shepherd came out of the gully, waved up his animals and left us, playing on his pipe.

Watching him going out of the *wadi*, Hassan said, 'I think they have been together.'

'No, I don't think so,' I replied. 'Perhaps she was looking for one of the animals.'

Hassan seemed to be unconvinced, for he said, 'Didn't you see her red face? You're still young.' He added, 'Why was the shepherd there in the gully?' Hassan smiled as we ended the talk about Kathra and went on playing in the sand as a prelude to work.

Some days later we came to the orchard as usual, but found an unknown man sitting under one of the trees. He had covered his head with his robe and was leaning against the grey trunk of the tree. As he saw us coming near he stood up and came towards us. We greeted him and he answered. We had not seen him before. He appeared grim and serious when he asked, 'Where is your father?'

'He's at home,' Hassan answered.

'Can I find him at home tomorrow?' asked the serious man.

'I don't know,' my brother answered.

'Please tell him that Bin Rafie will come to see him on an important matter tomorrow,' Bin Rafie said.

We promised him to do so. He thanked us and left, and disappeared behind the curves of the winding gully.

Kathra came a few minutes after he had left. She seemed to be more beautiful than she had been on any previous day. She was accompanied by her small brother. She tried to get us going at a certain game played with twenty-four small stones and another twenty-four different small stones, though we used instead of them the small and unripe fruit of figs. She did not join us in our game, but kept on looking towards the northern part of the gully, where the shepherd was sitting and beating the soil with his stick. Hassan seemed to be uninterested in the game that time, for he made many silly mistakes. I guessed that he was watching Kathra and the shepherd.

Next day we met Bin Rafie on a very beautiful red stallion with a white blaze. It had a black mane and tail. As the man passed us, he asked whether we had told our father, and we answered him that we had. We were anxious about that meeting, because we had not seen the man before. I turned my face and saw Bin Rafie going quickly along the wide road up a hill towards the tents of the tribe. I had heard about Bin Rafie as one of the generous and famous men in the Sawarkah tribe. I thought about his meeting with my father, but I could make nothing of it.

On the day after that, we were told by my father that he would follow us, and we had to prepare two baskets of grapes for him. My father came two hours after we had reached the orchard. We saw his brown mare tied near Abu Zaid's small house, and a few minutes later we saw the smoke coming up from Abu Zaid's home. We knew that coffee, at least, was being made for my father.

It was strange, because my father had seldom gone there before coming to see his beloved trees. Kathra did not come that day: she was busy because of my father's visit.

Some hours later my father came to us. He seemed to be unwilling to speak, so we brought the two baskets in silence and helped him to put them in the two panniers, one on each side of the horse. He left without talking, apart from a few words. Kathra did not come that day at all. Even the small boys did not come. I thought that something had happened at that meeting, but I could not make out what it was. I asked Hassan, but he provided no answer. We wished Kathra would come, but we left without having seen her, except a few times coming out of or going into their house.

In the evening I heard my father talking to my grandfather in one of the corners of the *Shik*. 'He has a rocky heart,' my father was saying. 'He roughly refused to get his daughter married to his nephew.'

'Didn't he give any reason for that?' my grandfather asked quietly.

'He said that Bin Rafie and the people of his tribe had once shifted from one place to another while he himself was absent. Abu Zaid was newly married, and had come in the evening, before sunset, to find that all the tents had beem moved except his. Seeing his tent alone, he was astonished. He asked his wife about the matter. She told him that she was waiting for the people to return for her. Soon enough, indeed, some men came with their camels. But Abu Zaid refused to let his tent be moved, in spite of the men's efforts. Early the next morning he left the place and came to where he is living now. In vain his brother, Bin Rafie, tried to persuade him to come back. Men of other tribes have tried, but they failed, too. Now his nephew, son of Bin Rafie, has seen his eldest daughter and loves her, but the hard-hearted man has refused consent. He said that his daughter would not love the son of a man who once insulted her father and mother, but he did not ask her whether she loves her cousin or not.' My father changed the pitch of his speech and began to talk in a low voice. 'I respect this man, but I see that he is too hard, almost black-hearted.'

'Don't worry! If the girl loves her cousin, the old man will change his ideas,' my grandfather said, while his teeth were holding the wooden stem of his pipe and his right hand was stirring the ashes of the tobacco in the bowl.

'But how,' asked my father, 'can he ever know that, when he's not going to ask his daughter?'

'He will do that sooner or later.'

I could not follow their speech to the end, because I was asked by some of the old men in the *Shik* to go and fill the jug with water. When I came back I found that the talk between my father and grandfather had already finished.

74

Time went on. The shepherd kept on coming daily, while we kept on watching him—suspiciously, because I had told Hassan what I had heard that one night. We wanted Kathra to come, so as to see the impression of love on her face. But she did not. We agreed to go to their house and to see her. When we went there we found that she was pale and, it seemed, sad. Abu Zaid was more thoughtful than any day before. He was sitting alone in the shade of his house.

The summer vacation ended and I went back to my school. I was busy preparing for the first term examinations. I did not remember Abu Zaid's family until I was told by Hassan that Bin Rafie's son had married Kathra a few months before I came back. It was said that Abu Zaid had sent some men to his brother, Bin Rafie, to tell him that he agreed to the marriage. It was said also, that my father had been the envoy.

The people found many explanations for Abu Zaid's change of decision: some said that he had felt that his nephew was worthy of Kathra and he would not find a better young man, while others attributed that change to the true love between the two young people, which was discovered at last by the old, grim man. Many other things were said, but the truth was within Abu Zaid's heart.

The people were puzzled when they saw Abu Zaid in his happiest mood on the day of his daughter's marriage. He proved to be a good horseman that day. His children were as happy as he. He accompanied the wedding-procession of his daughter till he was a mile or so from the place where his tribe was encamped. All became happier as they approached the tents. They were met by many men, women and children when they were some hundreds of yards from the tents. But all the people were surprised when they saw a horseman turn from the celebration and make his way back toward the east: the horseman was Abu Zaid. Some men tried to go after him, but they were forbidden by Bin Rafie, who said, 'Do not try the impossible: he would not come.'

The next summer we missed Kathra, and we had not seen the shepherd either. Abu Zaid was more active than before. I had seen him walking around the house, going in or out of the house, or doing some work in his vineyard. He invited my father many

**75**

times and kept on bringing him coffee when he found him busy. I had seen him more than once going down the gully, disappearing behind the curves; then after a while he used to return, following the same path. My brother told me that he had seen him once coming from that place when soon he was followed by Kathra, whose face was pale—pale, as we say, as a lemon.

Last summer I, civil servant in Saudi Arabia, was on a vacation. I had no place to go except the place where my parents now live. They were living alone. Some of my relatives were living near them. In the evenings sometimes they sat together in the shade of the small hut in which they now live. These relatives used to visit my parents from time to time.

One of those evenings there was a small meeting—my father, my uncle Abdulmalik, Salim Bin Salamah (he who once caught a thief), and some women and children. Their speech covered many topics, and as usual it went at last beyond the dreadful borders over to Wadi Al-Hisi, the life they had spent there, and the ways for going back to carry out what they had begun. They talked about our vineyard and about Abu Zaid.

As they came to this point, Salim asked my father, 'Is it true that Abu Zaid's son sent you money which his father borrowed from you before we were driven from our country?'

My father answered, 'No, but he sent me a letter telling me that he would send it just as soon as he received my answer. I had forgotten it: many years have passed since his daughter's marriage.'

'Have you the letter, father?' I asked.

'Yes. It's in the case where the documents and your certificates are to be found.'

I knew where these things were found. They were kept in a small old wooden box which had been in my father's possession for a very long time. I duly found the letter among many other papers: there were our educational certificates, and some documents which showed that my father had paid the taxes for his land and animals, and a drawing for the proposed modern farm, which was done nineteen years ago.

As I unfolded the letter, Salim and my uncle insisted that I should read it out to them. I looked at my father, who seemed to understand what I meant, because he said, 'Read it if they want.'

So I began to read :

*'Dear Mr Abdul Aziz,*

*I do not know whether you will receive this letter or not, but I shall follow it with another if I do not learn that you have received it. I am Ali, Abu Zaid's son. You may not remember me because I was small when we were driven out from our land. I think that it does not matter so much if you remember me or not. I want to tell you that four months ago my father became ill. It happened suddenly and we tried to bring him a doctor but he refused and told us that he hoped to be better the next day. One night his illness increased. My sister Kathra was on a visit to my father and in the morning she left the house and returned quickly and gave me three pounds and said, 'Take it and bring a doctor for my father." I knew that she had no money at all because the money which her husband earned was not enough even for their food and their three children.'*

The letter went on and on, not very well written, and I continued to read it aloud to Salim and my uncle Abdulmalik. But as I read, stumbling now and again over miswritten words, caught with some memory at the back of the throat or the mind, I began to pay less attention to the writing and more to what it conveyed.

Ali, then, had been about to ask Kathra where she got the three pounds, when he noticed that the gold piece which was hung on her neck was not there. The doctor, of course, gave them medicines and told them that their father would be better very soon. But days passed and Abu Zaid's health became worse.

He began to dream and to talk about things which were unseen. He talked about Wadi Al-Hisi, the wide road which led to the neighbouring village of Breer, and that he was going there to the market. They were all round him when, in one of his dreams, he said in a clear voice, 'Then they love each other? I thought that she did not love, even could not love, but there they are sitting close to each other. They're talking. Oof—his hands are on her shoulders ! She loves him and he must marry her.'

Abu Zaid seemed to be very tired when he asked for water to

drink. After Kathra had poured the water into his wide and dry mouth, he asked Ali to come near him. He took Ali's hand in his and said, 'My son, I know that I am leaving quickly for God's meeting, but I want to meet him pure and honest. I trust you to do what I will ask you. I borrowed forty pounds from Abdul Aziz Al-Diqs before the departure. I know that you have no money, but remember to send this amount of money to him as soon as you get it.'

He breathed a long sigh, and added, when he saw Kathra and the other children weeping, 'Do not weep, my dear children. I am not sorry for anything in life, except that I'm going to die before again seeing Wadi Al-Hisi. You must be happy because you are young and will go back and find that the vines have been waiting for you. Remember me when you sit under the big tree in front of our house.'

The voice of Abu Zaid became weaker and weaker, till they were unable to distinguish what he was saying. His eyes were open and a smile covered his face before his head fell silent on the pillow.

'*I mention all this only,*' I read out from the letter, '*because I feel that I am fulfilling the promise I gave to my father when I tell or write his last words. I worked day and night and Kathra helped me until I got the money, so I shall send it as soon as I receive your answer so as to be sure of your address. Please do not make me wait for a long time. Until I hear from you I remain thankful for your goodness and I am*
*Sincerely,*
*Ali.*'

While I was reading the letter, and for one moment afterwards, all the people were silent. Salim broke the silence to ask my father, 'What have you written to him?'

My father waited for a while, looked towards the west, and said, 'I wrote to him that his father had borrowed the money when we were on our land and that I will not take it back except upon our return.'

# CHAPTER 9

# *There Was the Time I Got Lost*

It was Monday evening. We were preparing ourselves to leave school the next day. Everyone was happy because he would meet parents, relatives and small friends. That evening I felt a greater longing to go home than at any time before. Perhaps most of the others, my schoolmates, had the same feeling. Everyone had his private dreams, but all these dreams were changed to unrestrained joy.

I slept only a few hours that night, while elder boys did not sleep at all. They knew that they had not to leave before breakfast, but still they could not sleep. They went on singing, though in low voices, in spite of the teacher's threats. They knew that he would not do anything before they left and that he would forget to punish them after the holiday. At last the teacher gave up in despair and went to sleep. Many years later I knew that the teacher might have had the same feeling as we had. He, in his turn, might have people waiting for his return. In addition to the people whom we longed for, he, perhaps, was longing for a lover.

Best clothes were worn the next morning. Many new, coloured garments were seen that day which had not been seen before, because white was the uniform. As a matter of habit the breakfast was prepared. The bell was rung and we lined up, then entered the dining-room. During breakfast one of the waiters came and told me that my uncle was waiting for me outside. I was very happy, because now I would return with him. He would tell me many things about our tribe—their place and the new things that had happened there.

The food on the long tables was left nearly untouched because of the glad and exciting moment. Only few cups of tea with milk were drunk. Not as usual, there was some noise. Everyone was talking with his neighbour. Some of the naughty boys, teasing the others whose turn it was to act as waiters that day, asked them to bring either tea or water and then did not drink any of it. Some of these acting waiters were annoyed, so they rebelled and refused to bring anything for those boys. It was their luck to be waiters that morning : if they had not been, they might have done the same as the other boys.

The cooks were laughing as they stood behind the partition and looked through the main hatch. I remember how Subri, an old one of them, came to the boy who was sitting opposite to me, leant down and whispered a few words in his ear. I did not know what he had said, but I guessed later that he had asked the boy to bring back some butter and dried milk, because I saw him carrying them when we returned three weeks later. Anyhow, I was luckier than my schoolmate, for I was asked by one of the teachers to buy some cow's butter for him. I brought him more than he had asked, and my father, who brought it to the school with me, refused to be paid for it in spite of the teacher's insistence. It was considered a present.

The bell, at last, was rung and we, the small boys, rushed in a crowd through the door. I could not help doing as the others. When I came out I stood near the door watching the boys as they passed. I was looking for Rabah, a boy from the neighbouring tribe, a little older than me. He came out, pushed by other boys. Before he was swept away I caught him by the sleeve of his robe. I said, as he turned to see who was catching at him, 'My uncle is waiting at the gate. Don't leave until we can leave together. I'll go to see him, then come back to fetch my bag.'

'Go and wait for me there, at the gate,' the boy said. 'I'll bring your bag. Give me the key. Let's go quickly.'

I was in a hurry like my friend Rabah, so I gave him the key to bring my already prepared bag. Then we both hurried : he rushed upstairs and I ran towards the main gate.

The path leading to the gate had already filled with leaving boys. They were leaving in small groups of two and three. These groups sometimes were broken by a boy rushing, like me. I could see my uncle's head near the gate, higher than all the small heads passing by him.

We kissed each other before shaking hands. 'What's up?' asked my uncle. 'Are you leaving for a holiday?'

'Yes,' I answered, 'it's the end of term.'

Some of the boys looked at us quickly as they passed, while the others had no time to do so. My uncle was looking curiously at the clean, small boys passing in front of him, perhaps to enrich his speech about his visit to the town after his return to the tribe.

'Where is your bag?' my uncle asked, smiling. 'Don't you have a bag like them?'

'Rabah, my friend, will bring it.' And I turned to see Rabah, moving heavily and trying to keep his balance with one bag in each hand.

'There he is, coming,' I said, as I rushed to help him. I introduced him to my uncle, who, it turned out, knew his father and some of his relatives. Then we all left. My uncle was in front and we two were a little behind him. In spite of the time we had spent at the gate we were not the last to leave. Some of the older boys, as tall as my uncle, were walking solemnly behind. Certainly they were happy, but it did not suit them to show their pleasure as children did. A few times I looked back and saw the long line following us. At the rear I saw three of the teachers, following us to the town.

I was disappointed, and so was my friend, when my uncle told us that we had to wait till the afternoon, because he had a long list of things to buy. We went after him to Jamiel Tork, a shop-keeper from whom the people of our tribe were accustomed to buy their things.

'Here you can put down your bags,' my uncle said as we reached the shop. Jamiel was busy selling to the people crowding in front of his piled, wooden counter. Inside the shop there were some bedouins, men and a few women. Some were sitting on old, low chairs, while others were sitting on the sugar and rice sacks. They felt at home in the shop, especially two old men who were smoking their pipes and talking in low tones and then laughing loudly. There was a wooden partition, behind which the women went. That was used as a store and sometimes used by the bedouins to deposit their luggage and collect their purchases before leaving.

Without asking permission my uncle raised the flap of the counter, and we followed him. I guessed that he really intended to stay for a long time, because he took the two bags and put them behind the partition.

'You can stay, or come with me,' he said.

I could not tell him that we wanted to leave and I felt that Rabah had the same idea. So I offered my help, hoping that this would shorten our waiting. My uncle got a crumpled paper out of his pocket and gave it to me. I saw a list of names, and near each there were the names of the things each needed : *Ali Bin Salamah —sugar and coffee. Saleh Abu Salman—four yards of white cloth and pepper. Wadha, his daughter—some perfume. Haj Ibrahim —coffee, sugar, carmundum.* Taleb, a young man who had married a few days before I last came to the school, was asking for a black dress for his wife, adding that it must be of the best kind.

Thus the list ran, till it covered nearly both sides of the paper. As I was reading the names I pictured the people whom they denoted, and I recognized my cousin's handwriting.

'You see it is difficult for you to buy any of them,' my uncle said. 'But you can help me by carrying the small bags and by reminding me of what I may forget.'

We were very glad to do anything, especially when it hastened our departure. He gave Jamiel the list and said, 'Mark the things that are to be found in your shop and get them ready before noon.'

Jamiel took the paper and began to put marks and to jot down on another paper the things he had marked. Then he gave the paper back to my uncle, who left the shop, followed by us. We stopped in front of many shops. Our load became heavier and heavier as we went down the long street, which had big, shady trees on both sides.

Seeing that we could carry no more, my uncle called a man driving a small cart. 'Put the bags in the cart,' my uncle told us, as the cart stopped near us in front of one of the shops.

We felt freer then. We saw some of our friends from school buying small presents for their families. Few were accompanied by relatives like us. Some of the boys were leaving and shouted to us merrily, as they passed in the crowded buses along that main street.

At three o'clock everything was ready. All the items were put in a huge cardboard box offered by Jamiel. It needed a big cart to carry it to the bus-station, and three men to get it down at the station, in addition to our humble help.

The station was full of passengers waiting for the buses. Despite its being so wide, people were crowding everywhere. Soon a bus came and the people made a rush, but, discovering that it was not the one going to Gaza, most of them returned and few jumped in. The main route was the one leading to Gaza. We were late, so we missed the bus that used to pass a few miles from our tribe. So we had to take the Gaza bus, then take the bus to Faloja, where we could leave the heavy things we had, to be fetched by someone from the tribe the next day.

Rabah and I felt disappointed because we were going to arrive late. In my heart I wished that my uncle had not come that day : then we would have been in our tribes by this time. My uncle seemed to be disappointed, too, probably because of the trouble that he would face in moving the carton from the rack of one bus to another. Maybe he felt that it was he who had delayed us, for he began to amuse us by making some jocular comments. We laughed, but, I think, not for long.

Two buses for Gaza came and left without our being able to catch either of them. The box was the cause. We had to put it on first, but the bus would not wait till the job was done.

The third bus came, and it was said that it would be the last one that day. So we insisted on going by it.

'One of you,' said my uncle, 'must get inside and reserve a seat, and I, helped by the other, will deal with the box.'

I was chosen for the first job, because Rabah was able to help more than me. It was very difficult to find my way among the shouldering men, so I stood close behind a fat man. Driven by the others I found myself inside the bus, unable to find a seat even for myself. I looked here and there, but there was no hope. There, outside the bus, I saw my uncle's box ascending. Then I was unable to see anything outside. I glimpsed my uncle getting up with the crowd but I could not see Rabah, which I attributed to his being short. A few minutes later, the bus—which had never switched off its engine—pulled out, and I could see the trees, which seemed to be moving along with the bus. Soon the bus was passing our school, then the cemetery.

My uncle was in front of me—six or seven men in front. He was looking ahead, and I expected that Rabah would be in front of him. I was standing, but I did not feel tired because I was so happy at returning.

Some of the passengers rang the bell by pulling the stretched rope, and when the bus stopped they got down. As soon as one got down, the nearest would take his place. Thus the crowd became less and less as we went forward. My uncle found a seat nearly in the middle of the trip. I had not seen Rabah : perhaps he had found a place somewhere and I could not see him. I myself, about half an hour later, found a seat.

The sun was setting as we came near Gaza. Some seats were empty, because most of the passengers were either bedouins living near the road or villagers whose villages were on the road. I wondered why my uncle did not turn round : he was looking ahead all the time.

Two miles before we reached Gaza my uncle pulled the bell, and I wondered why he had done so. The bus stopped and I stood up and followed my uncle. I did not see Rabah. My uncle turned his face to pick a paper bag from one of the shelves and to my great surprise he was not my uncle. He was exactly like my uncle : there was no difference between them except in the face.

The man got down and I returned, not to my seat but to look for my uncle. I examined every face in the bus, but neither Rabah nor my uncle was there. There were not many people in the bus. Three of them were bedouins, of whom two got down a few minutes later.

I was puzzled what to do. It was my first experience of being in a town without company. I had money, but I could not do anything with it. I did not think of the morning, but of the night that I was going to spend. Where should I go? Should I go to an hotel? I had no idea of hotels, apart from that one when I was accompanied by my father. It was evening and the electric lamps were being lit : they lit up, then were quickly turned off and relit more than once, and finally all of them, on both sides of the street, were lit and stayed lit. Their light could not remove my feelings of melancholy, as the bus went up the road through Sajaia, one of the Gaza quarters.

The only bedouin left in the bus got down and, without thinking of what I was doing, I got down and followed the man. He had nothing in his hands, but I had my bag. I had to walk quickly so as to keep close to that man. I felt completely strange in the town and could not make up my mind where I had to go. I had passed through Gaza a few times, but as a small child. I did not remember the streets I had passed through.

Sometimes the man was clear to me in the light of a lamp, then nearly disappearing as he entered the shadow. I hurried till I was almost on his heels. The man did not feel that someone was pursuing him. I thought about what I should say to him and the manner of my address. He might not care about my situation—then what should I do?

Anyhow I felt that I had no choice but to say, 'Good-evening, uncle.' The man turned his head to see whether it was he who was being addressed or not. Seeing me looking at him, the man said, 'Good-evening, boy.'

'I have lost my uncle and I don't know where to go.'

'Who are you? And where do you come from?' the man enquired.

I told him my full name as if I were telling it to a new teacher to register it in the marks notebook. And I told him how I had missed my uncle and my friend Rabah.

The man took me away to the pavement, because a car was passing close to the place I was standing. 'Don't you know any people here?' he asked.

'No, I don't.' I could not remember anyone at that moment.

'Follow me, son.'

He went on and I followed him. On the way he told me that we were going to an hotel and added that he would accompany me to the station and put me on the Faloja bus. He comforted me by saying that we might meet my uncle the next morning.

I do not remember what the outside of the hotel was like, because all that I remember is that we entered a house. 'Here is the hotel,' the man said.

He ascended the stairs and I followed him—now I was lighter because he had already insisted on carrying the bag. When we finished the stairs, we came directly to a big hall with grand armchairs. On the chairs there were a few people sitting: some were drinking tea or coffee and talking, while others were just talking. In one of the corners of the hall there was a counter, and behind it there was a bald man with glasses. My friend went up to him and talked with him. He gave his name and asked me to give mine. After registration the bald man stood up, took a key and waved to us to follow him.

'Here is your room,' the bespectacled, bald man said. 'You can take your rest.'

My friend put down the bag and asked me to choose one of the beds. I sat on one of them and began to think of my uncle. My friend interrupted my thinking by saying, 'Do you want to eat?'

'No, thank you.'

'I think you're in need of a cup of tea.'

I was really in need of nothing except to go home. So I thanked him and refused.

'Now,' he said, 'I'm going to see some friends. You can sleep, and in the morning I'll come to take you to the bus-station.'

Before the man reached the hall, I had already followed him and asked him if he knew Abu Hassira's family. For I had remembered that there was a family of this name who knew my father and some other people of our tribe.

'Don't you know where they live?' he asked.

'No, I don't, but I heard that they are near the sea.'

He asked the bald man, who said he could not help. He thought a little, looked at me and said, 'Since you insist on following me, let us try.'

He offered the bald man money, which was refused, and I took my bag and followed him. We passed through many side-streets. I had no idea where we were going. Occasionally he stopped to make enquiries. Some people told him that they did not know the name, while others laughed at us and went on their way. We walked for more than an hour without finding anyone who could give us directions.

While we were walking we passed by some gypsies dancing and singing. Some of them knew my friend and invited him to stay, but he refused. I wondered how they came to know him, but then he told me that they had passed by his tribe while they were roaming and that he had been kind to them.

We had not walked far after that before a man told us the place, and not long afterwards we came to the house which he had described. It was not far from the sea, surrounded on all sides by trees. I could smell the sea smell and hear the sound of the waves.

My friend knocked on the door, but no one answered. Then he knocked loudly. A boy came out and, finding us strangers, went in again. He came back with a man who welcomed us and led us to a room with carpets only, without chairs. On one side of that room there was an old man who seemed to be blind. I felt that as I shook hands with him.

The coffee was got ready. After it was served my friend told them his name, my name and my story. The man and his two sons who were there at that moment welcomed me more and more.

'Now I have to leave,' my kind friend said, standing up. In vain they tried to persuade him to spend the night as their guest. He shook hands with the old man and his sons, with me, and then left. I went with him to the door to thank him. I am glad I did that—though, indeed, it was not very much for a fairly polite, rather small boy to do. I am sorry that I have forgotten my bedouin's name : I think it was Ahmed, but all I am sure of is that then I was young enough, tribal enough, not to see his behaviour as so very exceptional.

When my friend had left, the old man shouted for his wife, who came directly. He told her about me. The old woman kissed me and sat close to me.

'Don't you remember, Khadija,' the old man said to his wife, 'the happy times we spent when we visited his grandfather and grandmother? He was not born then, even his mother was still a child playing with the lambs in front of the tent.'

'Yes, I do. I'll not forget those days. They are kind people,' the wife said.

The small children sat near their grandmother and began to listen to their grandfather's talk. A memory led to a memory as the night went on. I felt at home among these people. I grew sleepy, and my small neighbours were already asleep while the talking went on, sometimes by the old blind man and at others by his old wife.

I do not know how much I slept that night, but for sure it was little. In the morning one of the old man's sons accompanied me to the bus-station, after a warm farewell from Abu Hassira's family. He helped me to get in the Faloja bus. He was waving to me as the bus went. At one of the crossroads the bus stopped, and I saw my uncle and Rabah standing by the enormous cardboard box.

87

# CHAPTER 10

# *That Old Man in Room Nine*

I CAN still remember my mother saying to my father, when he used to be extravagant when he had guests, 'Nassralla, God bless him, used to say: "If it is to be done once only, then I will spend all that I have." ' Last summer it was I who said that to her when I had invited some friends. But this time she said, 'God rest his soul, he may be happy now. He is lucky that he died before he could see our present troubles. He lived on the earth he loved, and died there.'

Nassralla's image did not depart from my mind that day. It took me eighteen years backward. Everything was as clear to me as if it had been taking place at the time.

Nassralla was an old man. He was short and thin, but healthy. His grey beard belied the activity he had. He was a pleasant man and we, the children then, found him amicable. He used to make jokes whenever he met any of us: sometimes he imitated a dumb man, and at others he imitated other old and serious men. He was busy all the time, or seemed to us so.

Many places and things were known by his name—'Nassralla's orchard', 'Nassralla's figs', 'Nassralla's houses' and 'Nassralla's mare'. The last was the best known to us, because we could hardly ever see him without his beautiful white horse. There was a useless part of his land, full of small gullies and the wild thorn plants, which he changed to a productive vineyard. The gullies became filled with eucalyptus trees and sometimes with figs. He did most of the work himself. It was a normal scene to see him making a small hole in the ground, with his white mare grazing not far from him.

Once we were coming back from school in the afternoon, playing and sometimes running, happy as we always were on leaving school in the afternoons. We saw Nassralla's white horse, black-tailed, grazing the dry grass calmly, not far from the road and near one of the bigger gullies. In spite of our passing that gully daily on our way to school, we used to feel a kind of loneliness there, especially when alone. No one passed through that deep gully unless he had something to do—to look, probably, for a lost sheep or cow. Because of the sandy soil, the gully had become deeper and deeper as time went on. As we drew near we recognized the horse and we glady expected to see Nassralla, though it would be a strange thing to see him there. We knew that the gully was on his land, but wondered why he had come there.

The road passed along the edge of the gully. We looked down into it, but could not see Nassralla there. Then we heard some faint thuds. We went to the place where the sound came from and saw Nassralla holding his mattock in his hands as he stood looking at the small hole he had made in the ground. As he saw us he said, 'You have come at a suitable time. Come and let me see how you can dig more.'

We hastened to help him. We were about to quarrel over who would work with the new mattock, while Nassralla was laughing at us one moment and encouraging us at the other. Really, we did nothing for him, but damaged the hole he had already done. His face was as pleasant as it usually was, when he took the mattock to re-make what we had spoiled. The sun was about to set when we went out from the gully with Nassralla, and before we reached his horse he told us that the next year we would see the green figs and eucalyptus growing healthy there, and that we would no more fear to come down that small valley.

'Now,' he said, 'the one who reaches the horse first I'll let ride pillion behind me till we reach the tribe. Stand in a line! Now— one, two, three!' Within seconds Hassan was holding the halter-rope of the mare and shouting, 'I've beaten them, grandfather.' Hassan was not Nassralla's grandson, but we all used to call him so, as with other respected old men. So Hassan rode pillion to Nassralla, while Mohammed, his grandson, walked with us behind the horse which went slowly along the road towards the tribe.

Three years passed. I was at the Beer Al-Saba school, working hard so as to be top of the class and realize my father's hope of becoming a famous engineer. I did well and was getting very good results, except in drawing, in which I was about to fail. Once I had forgotten my pencil and the teacher punished me, so since that time I hated drawing and its teacher.

I used to hate Monday because we had drawing, so it was one Monday in the morning when I pretended to be ill and asked for a chit for the doctor. There were another three boys who went with me, and I did not know whether they were really sick or if they were pretending as I was. There were many people at the hospital. As I entered the doctor's room my heart was beating, it seemed to me, rapid and loud. I was afraid that the old, busy doctor might discover my trick and write to the headmaster, who would punish me. He ordered me to bare my breast to his stethoscope, and then wrote down a few English words, which I could not understand as they were written in that joined type of handwriting I had not yet learnt.

'To the hospital,' he said quickly. I looked at the man at the door who might know that I did not know where to go, and indeed he pointed to help me and delivered me to a young nurse. She led me along the long corridors of the hospital. She was holding me by the hand as she entered a very clean room with a big, white table at which was an old, grey-haired, bespectacled nurse. My name was written down and I was told that I had to sleep in room Number Six. I was struck by that, for it was the first time that I was going to sleep in a hospital. I smelt the smell of medicines, and imagined sick people dying. I wished that I had joined the drawing class. It was God's punishment for my crime.

I asked the nurse who was leading me to this appointed room whether I could go back to my school, but she told me that it was better for me to stay at the hospital and not to be afraid. She may have known me to be a stranger, because we had a special uniform at that school, by which all the people of the town knew us. That might be the reason for her kindness. I told her that I had begun to feel well there and then, but she told me that those were the doctor's orders and they had to be obeyed. I saw there was no chance of my going back, and, in spite of my feeling of loneliness and anxiety, I followed the nurse to enter the room where it had been decided that I was to stay. It was a room with three beds, two having children in them, while the third stood empty, clean, neat and white.

The smiling nurse showed me the clothes locker, ordered me to undress and showed me the bathroom. The two small children were pleased when they saw me, and I learnt that they were going to leave the hospital in a few days. I began to feel that I was really sick, because of the strong smell of the rooms and the feeling that I might spend nights here before I could return to school.

I spent the first night and I had a lot of mixed dreams. They were fearful ones, so I was very glad the next morning when I awoke to find that all that I had seen were just dreams. After breakfast Ragheb, one of the two children, asked me to follow him to the garden where we could meet an old bedouin man who used to tell him, and other children in the hospital, many amusing and strange stories about the bedouin life. He told me that the old man was not seriously sick, but complaining of a small wound in the tip of his big toe. No one came to visit him except a young, short and well-dressed bedouin, who kept on visiting at intervals. He was called Mosa, he was very kind to them, and he had brought him a very nice toy : this he showed me.

'I have not seen the bedouin tents, but I would like to visit this old man when he goes out,' Ragheb said in a passionate voice. 'I'm very sorry I'll leave before seeing Mosa, his son, but I will come again to visit the old man with my father.'

I was anxious to see this old man, because I felt that I would feel friendly with him, to see if he was worthy of Ragheb's praise, and to hear these amusing stories, as the boy called them. When we came into the garden Ragheb shouted. 'There he is!' And shouted louder, 'My grandfather! Grandfather!'

A few yards away and on an old chair I saw Nassralla, smaller than I was used to seeing him, and dressed completely in white. His face was pale and there was no place for the smile which was considered one of his facial features. He looked at me for a while and then he shouted, 'Isaak, my dear boy—who brought you here?' As he said this and rose, I ran to meet him because I saw that he was limping.

He took me by the hand and called me to sit near him on the

bench. I was looking at his white-wrapped right foot, while Ragheb was still standing at the spot where he had shouted to Nassralla. Nassralla called him, and he came and sat beside me. Nassralla kept his face up while he was talking, but I saw him passing his sleeve across his eyes before my eyes could reach his tired ones. I did not see their usual sparkle, but they were green and yellow and looked as if they were made of glass.

He told me how the mattock had wounded his toe when he was moving the soil around the trees. He did not pay attention to the matter at first, then, seeing that it became more and more painful and apparently serious, his son and Haj Ibrahim asked him to go to the dispensary in the neighbouring village, where he might find a medicine. The nurse there had told him that it was beyond his control and it would be better to go to Gaza or Beer Al-Saba, where he could find better nursing and cleverer doctors.

'I asked them not to come with me,' Nassralla said, in a low voice. 'They insisted on that, but I refused—they have a lot of things to do. It was necessary that just one would come with me, and that is why I agreed to Mosa leaving his work and coming here. Yesterday I asked him to leave me and to go back to the tribe, so as to assure the people that I am well and they have not to bother themselves by visiting me.' Nasralla looked at me then and added, 'Your grandfather, Haj Ibrahim, asked Mosa not to tell you about the matter should he happen to come across you. It is fate that brings us together. I am very glad to see you—but have you anything wrong?'

I felt my fault and I was ashamed to tell him that the only thing I had wrong with me was pretence. I felt also that I could not tell him lies, so I just said, 'I am well now and I do not feel anything.' I had been afraid of the hospital, but I felt at home with Nassralla and Ragheb, who stayed silent all the time. Soon afterwards Ragheb asked Nassralla to tell us a new story, and the old man seemed to me reluctant, despite his low voice beginning to tell a strange story which I had never before heard him tell.

It was about an old woman who had a child. She was very poor, but she worked very hard to educate him. She was proud of him when he became a promising young man. The son felt his mother's troubles and her sympathy for him, so he left his mother and went to work in a far off place. She awaited his letters for a long time, but in vain. She did not receive a line. At last a man came to tell her that he had a letter for her. She was at the zenith of happiness when he opened the letter and told her that it was a letter of condolence: her son had died. The poor old woman had been blind since that time.

It was not of Nassralla's nature to tell such sad stories. Ragheb was as disappointed as me. Soon after he finished the story, the smiling nurse who had brought me the day before came to tell us that we had to go inside, because the doctor was about to come. Nassralla promised to meet us in the afternoon in the garden and to tell us a very nice story—Abu Zaid and his adventures in Morocco and Tunis.

When the doctor came and found that I had nothing wrong with me, he looked at the nurse and said, 'You are right.' Turning his kind face to me, he added, 'You are well now, my dear boy, and you can leave today.' Then he left the room, followed by the nurse. A few minutes later she came back and told me to put on my clothes and follow her, so as to take a paper for the headmaster of the school as an excuse for my absence. I asked her if I could go and see Nassralla before leaving. She caught me by the hand and brought me inside his room.

He was in a room bigger than the one I had been in. There were six beds and they were full of men. I saw Nassralla sitting with his face clasped against his knees. He raised his head when I called as I came near him. He smiled when I told him that I was about to leave, and said, 'I hope that you will visit me on Fridays. You may meet Mosa next Friday.' When I was leaving, I tried to insist on his not getting up, knowing the pains he suffered, but he went with me till the end of the corridor that led from his room.

I went on alone to my room to bid Ragheb farewell, but I found him not there, though his things were there still. Seeing that it was of no use to wait longer, I left first the room, then the hospital, and went along the street to the right. But, before I had passed the hospital, I heard Ragheb calling me. He was at our place of the morning in the garden. There was a low wall on which there were black bars. A man could see into the garden, but it was very difficult for me to do that, so I was satisfied just to see Ragheb's face and to ask him if he wanted anything brought from the town. But he thanked me and told me he wanted nothing, and I left for the school.

On the next Thursday I thought of going to Nassralla in the hospital, despite my knowing that it was forbidden to go down to the town except on Fridays. In the afternoon, when lessons were over, I tried to get out by the green-barred gate, till I saw that the door-keeper was sitting on his chair at that main gate. I thought of going over the small wall which was between our school and the neighbouring wood. I knew that I had to go west, pass through the forest, turn north and cross the road on my way to the hospital. Realizing it was late for all this, I gave up the idea and waited till the next morning.

Early in the morning, after having my breakfast, I left the school with Ahmad, my close friend, for the hospital. We arrived there at nearly seven. I rushed along with my friend, who insisted on carrying our simple presents to my old relative as a symbol of his friendship. There were many people inside, come to visit their relations, and it was difficult for one to make one's way. When we reached the room where Nassralla was, we saw that it was crowded with visitors. Every bed was surrounded by a group of people—men, women and some small children. There was no one near Nassralla's bed and he was alone in it, with his eyes apparently fixed on the door. Marks of pleasure came over his face when he saw me with my small bedouin friend. All the people with him in the room were from the town, so we—yes, the three of us—seemed different from the people around us.

I asked Nassralla about his foot and he told me that he felt happy now. I knew that it had become worse, because I noticed a clean and smooth stick nearby, leaning against the wall by the bed-head. He told me that he was anxious because Mosa had not come, and thought that something must have happened or he would have come again.

It was about ten, the time to end visits, when the people began to leave the room one by one. We were the last to leave, but, just before leaving, we heard a noise outside and there was a great crowd from our tribe—many men, a few women and two children, Nassralla's grandsons.

The joy and happiness were mixed with pain and sadness on all their faces, apart from the two children who annoyed me by their silly questions. I learnt that the people had not been allowed to enter at first, but Dr Ali Atawnah, a bedouin doctor at the hospital, knowing their difficult situation, persuaded the authorities to let them come in. I heard the people praising him more than once during that short visit. After an hour, the permitted time, Dr Ali came and the people knew that they had to leave, so we went, all of us, and Nassralla was left alone.

When we were outside they became aware of me for, it would seem, the first time. My father told me many things about my mother and my brothers. My grandfather, Haj Ibrahim, asked me and Ahmad to go with them for dinner, but I told them that we were not allowed to stay longer and we ought to have our dinner at school. He smiled, and turned his face towards the other people as if he were going to tell them that life inside the town differed from the life outside. I greeted them all before leaving, but my father followed me and asked me if I was in need of money. I told him that I had enough, but he insisted on giving me four pounds, of which my grandmother had given him two as a gift for me.

In the afternoon of the next day I climbed the small wall, passed the small wood and made my way to the hospital. As I was walking along the street leading to it, I was afraid of meeting any of my teachers by chance—and indeed it would be a calamity if the headmaster should see me. So I kept on walking quickly near the walls and looking sideways and backwards and thinking every man with a red fez might be the headmaster and so continually avoiding anyone with a fez. When I reached the wall of the hospital, I could not see anyone there. Seeing a stone not far off, I rolled it close to the wall and climbed on to it. It enabled me to see more, but indeed there was no one except for a cook.

When the cook saw me, she told me to go away, thinking I was playing, but I begged her to call the patient Nassralla, an old bedouin in Room Nine. She refused at first, but, seeing the eagerness on my face and knowing that I was not of the town, she went inside and then came back to tell me that he would come soon. I was afraid that one of the teachers would pass by, and then my crime would be a double one : I was regarded as a calm and polite boy, and climbing a wall would bring shame even to the school as a whole.

The arrival of Nassralla broke into these excited black

thoughts. He seemed sadder than before, despite his welcoming smile. He told me that it was not good for me to come without permission, but I told him that I would have it the next time, in spite of my knowing that would be impossible. He told me that he insisted upon Mosa not coming back but staying away to take care of their land, small children and animals, because he was the eldest son and he ought to take the responsibility during his father's absence. He told me that perhaps I would see the people again the next Friday. I asked if I could bring anything for him from the town. He thanked me, but refused the offer with a smile.

I left him and went back to the school, more afraid than before because I imagined that someone might have seen me. When I climbed over the wall round the wood, I saw no boys in the courtyard of the school. Everything was silent. I felt a great fear. My limbs began shaking. I guessed what was wrong: someone had seen me and told the headmaster. It happened the very few times when one of the students was seen in the town: the bell used to be rung and the boys were gathered in the classrooms and the absentees were checked. Their punishment was known: for one month or more they were forbidden to go down to the town.

I came to my classroom, but found that my name had already been written as absent, and I was led to the headmaster's room. Without asking me where I had been, he pronounced, 'You, too! Two weeks! Do not do it again!'

I left the room and found that the boys had already gone out to the playground. I learnt that two naughty boys had been seen by the headmaster himself in the town, and I learnt that they were now deprived of going down to the town till the end of that term. I knew then that I had not been seen, but, despite that, I made up my mind not to go again till the next Friday.

On Wednesday afternoon I was called by some boys to see a man asking about me at the gate. I ran there quickly and saw Mosa with his black robe and a case in his hand. After greeting me, he asked me when I had last seen his father. I told him, and said I was sorry that I would be unable to do it again. He told me that Nassralla had been shifted to a hospital in Bethlehem, and added that he was anxious because the faces of the nurses at the hospital were not encouraging. He had decided to go back to the tribe and tell them about the matter; then he would go to look for his father in the hospitals of Bethlehem.

He was in a hurry, so he bade me farewell and left. I stood at the gate. I stood in the same place where I had stood when for the first time I saw my father go down the long street to disappear in the town. And this time, too, I was sad.

Two months went by, and I was very pleased because it was a spring vacation. It was of only three weeks, but it was going to be both very pleasant and interesting, for I would be able to play on the new, green grass, see the newborn animals, the green fields of barley and wheat, and join the shepherds in their happy games.

When I reached the tribe, I found everything as I had expected: nature was awakening, all creatures were full of life, the happy homecoming was about to be repeated. I began to plan for a full holiday. I went to the *Shik* so as to greet the men there. Seeing my grandfather, Haj Ibrahim, and Mosa, I remembered Nassralla. As I shook hands with Mosa I enquired about his father. He answered, with a touch of sadness on his face, 'He has died—God rest his soul.' 'God rest his soul,' was repeated by most of the people in the *Shik*.

I understood later that Nassralla had died in a hospital in Bethlehem—had died as an unknown man there, and been buried in a humble grave in a small cemetery on the southern side of that town. I passed more than once by that gully where I had seen Nassralla that time. The trees were high and green, but Nassralla was not there to see them. He had left them to his sons and grandsons and gone to another world.

I do not know whether the trees are still green and high as they were. Eighteen years have passed. But I like to picture them green and high as Nassralla left them.

# CHAPTER 11

# *The Bare Earth*

FOURTEEN years ago there was a group of old, ragged tents at the bottom of Kanar mountain on the road leading from Dura to Hebron. They were not far from that road which was built by the Turks during the First World War. It was almost unused by cars since a new, asphalted one had been constructed. Not far from the other side of the road there is Kanar Spring, from which what remained of our flocks and herds used to drink. The spring was so old that no one was able to tell its age, because it had been known by fathers and forefathers. Those old, ragged tents were ours, as well as those few animals. In spite of being ragged and old, they were still better than the refugee camps, and we, despite our great misery, felt better than those people who were accustomed to the life in modern towns and found themselves suddenly in tents without water, electricity and other necessary things.

The animals we had were killed by the cold weather and by snow. I still remember how these poor sheep and cows died in dozens while their owners stood looking at them, being unable to do anything for them. The great number of animals that died led the people to give death no importance. The important thing was how to get rid of these corpses. People were forced to stable their free-ranging beasts in the old Roman caves so as to avoid the increasing snow, but still death could not be stopped. It followed the miserable animals even into those old, deserted caves.

When spring came, our tribe had no animals except those remnants to drink from Kanar Spring that year. People became really aware of what cold weather in the mountains meant, and the few animals left began to acclimatise themselves to this kind of weather, but still they decreased every year and became a heavy responsibility which could not be thrown off easily. That was why the people were trying to find a better place. Wadi Al-Hisi, the place which they had never left before, was beyond their reach. The good, faithful earth on both its banks had become no more the place of peace and fertility. The earth which collected the people and kept them together was stolen.

Life had become very difficult, but still it was dear and worth living. People began for the first time to feel that they had to struggle for life. The bare mountains near Kanar were not suitable for their settlement. They had to look for another place, where they could get food for their children and their remaining animals.

So a melancholy mood came over the people. As children we were able no more to enjoy our games, except on a few occasions. We, too, were feeling that there was something wrong. The happiness we had enjoyed by the banks of Wadi Al-Hisi no longer existed. There were no games at night and no merry runs on the dewy grass. The green cornfields, the new vineyards and citrus orchards were far. Nassralla's figs and eucalyptus trees were beyond our reach. Everything was changed for the worse and we, the children, felt that.

The men of our tribe used to meet in my uncle's tent, because my grandfather, Haj Ibrahim, had died in the very year we were driven from Wadi Al-Hisi and people insisted on taking his tent as the *Shik* in respect for his memory. The sound of the old *mihbash* pounding the coffee beans could still be heard early in the morning, in the evening, and sometimes at different times—it might be noon or late at night, according to the time that a guest did come. But I could feel the change of the *mihbash* sound. Oda was still the man who crushed the coffee, but his happy, musical beats were not the same. He had been able to make us dance to his *mihbash* rhythm, but now he did the job as a matter of course, and, as I think now, it expressed the sad emotion deeply suppressed in his soul. Ziadi, the bard, had disappeared, and many different tales were told about his fate : some people said that he had died in the war, others claimed that he had left for the east bank of Jordan, while others said that he was wandering between Syria and Iraq. Really, he was seldom mentioned, because the men had many other, and more important, things to discuss.

One of these important things was whether to stay in Kanar's bare mountains, near Dura and Hebron where there were schools for boys and girls, or to go to the eastern side of Nablis where people could find something to work at and a better place for the animals that remained, and where they could find schools, but not so near as the Hebron ones. The matter was discussed nearly every night, but no decision was taken. My father and a few others supported the idea of staying, while most of the tribe favoured going. Each party was trying to convince the other, but still no decision was reached. The rumour of the departure was heard among the women and they were all afraid of getting the tribe separated by this unwelcome departure. The children heard the discussions and felt that there was no necessity in the world to justify that departure if it would lead to separation.

It was one night in autumn when a great number of the men, nearly all the men, were gathered in the *Shik*. The coffee beans had been roasted and the sound of the *mihbash* was heard: it seemed to me louder than before, perhaps to call those who had not yet come. But the men were silent. The coffee was drunk and few words were spoken. I saw some women coming to the women's part of the tent. There was something going to happen. I had never seen such a great collective suspense. Everything was serious—even Ali, the smiling man, was serious too that night.

'Winter is coming very soon and we have to decide. Otherwise it will kill the rest of the animals,' Saleh Bin Aqiel, one of the old men, said.

'Yes,' said another, 'there are few days left and it is better to decide as soon as possible.' He then turned to my father and asked, 'What have you to say, Abdul Aziz?'

My father was silent and, it seemed, deeply thinking. I could not tell what kind of thoughts were in his mind, because he raised his head to the question as if he had come from another, distant world.

'I have no more to say than what I said last night. Everyone has to act as he likes. I see that most of you are wanting to leave, and I would like to leave with you—but I must stay. My son Ibrahim will go with you and take with him the sheep and cows that I have, but I must stay here because of the school for my sons. I do not want to interrupt their studies.'

'That is not a convincing reason. There are schools in Nablis, and we shall all send our children there. We don't want to separate,' Saleh said.

'I feel pessimistic about this departure. I prefer to stay here in these bare mountains rather than to depart—and you will have my son with you. It is better for you to go tomorrow to Hebron and get trucks to carry you to wherever you want to go.' Then he turned to my brother and said, 'It is the first time that I separate from the tribe, but I feel that I have to do so. Tomorrow go with the people and get a car for your tent and go with the tribe.'

Seeing my father's determination to stay they agreed upon the way of departure, partly because they were obliged to do so and partly because they knew that my father was going to live in Dura, the neighbouring village. At last the decision had been taken, and Sunday of the next week was appointed as the day of departure. The rest of the night was spent in speaking about the preparation and aftermath of departure. Soon men and women began to leave the tent, and silence came again except for occasional barking from the still unaware dogs.

Knowing what would happen a few days later, we boys began to play our old games. But we could not bring any one of them to an end. In spite of being very young, we realized what the departure would mean. The talks of men at night became longer, but they were lacking the joy they had had before.

The days passed quickly, and it was Saturday evening when all the men were sitting round the faintly burning fire. The sound of my grandfather's *mihbash* was heard for the last time in Kanar's mountains. Shehdi, my cousin, was crushing the coffee that night. He was known as the best one at making the *mihbash* send out its best musical sounds. He was looking westward, perhaps thinking of Wadi Al-Hisi. His eyes were motionless as stones and the muscles of his face were set like those of a statue. The beats were regularly done and I could hear them sad and faint, as if they were reflecting the inner feeling of the silent men sitting round the fire. The coffee pots were standing near the fire, as usual. No one could tell exactly where they would be the next night. The coffee was drunk and few words were spoken. Everyone was feeling that it was the last night for them with a man who had spent his whole life with them, a man who was the son of their dead sheikh : but he had chosen, and they could not change his mind.

101

We did not play that night, but we sat in a big circle round the faint lamp of Om Mutair, an old woman, who told us some old tales about ancient Arabian tribes and their wars. We did not leave her tent until the young moon sank behind Kanar's high mountain. All the boys left her, and I led off my young brothers, Idris and Yahia, and went home. Hearing our return, my grandmother, who was going to leave the next day, came out of her tent and called us. She asked us to sit for a while with her. Then she said, 'Tomorrow we shall depart. I may not see you again. I am too old and may die before being able to see you educated young men. I shall be proud then.' She sighed, and added, 'Be kind to your mother and bear in mind that she will be living as a stranger just for your sake.'

Then she took a small wooden box and got out three pieces of gold and gave a piece to each one as a gift. We took the gold-pieces, and left her after she had kissed us.

Early on Sunday morning people began to prepare for their move. Everyone was busy and even we took part in that action. Men were putting the tents and the other heavy things into the cars, while women and children were doing the light jobs—small cases, mattresses and cooking-pots. Shouts were heard everywhere, those of the people mixed with the noise of animals too young to have gone with the cattle which had left earlier in the morning, being unable to cover that long distance between Kanar and Nablis.

Three of the drivers were standing in front of one of the big cars. They were drinking the tea which I, ordered by my father, had brought to them as they were smoking their cigarettes. They laughed when they saw an old woman—Om Mutair, our narrator of the previous night—running after one of her hens. The hen was running round the lorry where the drivers were standing. Being tired and ashamed, the poor old woman began to mutter low words which I could not catch, but I guessed that they would be a kind of complaint. Then she stood, as if she were thinking of leaving the hen and sparing herself all these troubles. Seeing her confusion and angry with those rude laughing drivers, I put down the tea-pot and ran after the hen, which went under the car. But I followed it and, helped by the old woman and one of the drivers (perhaps made repentant by me, perhaps basically kind-hearted),

I caught the hen and gave it to Om Mutair, who took it and went to the car where her things were.

Nearly everthing now had been put in, and the drivers began to complain of having their trucks overloaded. The small children were careless of all that was happening around them. They got into the cars and began to play in them, climbing on the high sides and calling to each other.

At last it was the farewell moment. My father was standing on the bare piece of land where the *Shik* had been removed. Embraces and kisses were the marks of this farewell. I still remember how everyone bade him farewell. Ali, one of the most amiable men, turned his face away quickly after embracing my father. He did not speak any of the usual words, but murmured words which, I thought, no one could grasp.

'I have not known you so, Ali,' my father said. 'We must face it as men do. There is a stronger tie! It is the earth there, in Wadi Al-Hisi.'

Ali did not wait till the end of my father's speech. Putting his robe over his head (as men are wont to do for protection under a very great sun), shrouded, concealed, he left for the car.

Not far from this spot there was the women's farewell. There were some tears there. The children stopped shouting, perhaps felt for the first time that it was not a matter of a short trip. I myself tried to say goodbye to those people I liked, but it was late because the engines of the cars had already been started. My grandmother, who had just left my mother, came quickly towards me. She bent over, kissed me, and I felt her hot tears on my cheeks. Then she left.

Our small family—I, my parents and young brothers—were standing as the cars left. There were many waves and I was unable to follow them all, so I kept my eyes on the car of Grandmother and Cousin Shehdi. Soon the cars disappeared behind the trees in one of the Kanar curves. We were alone.

And it was the first time that I saw our tent alone, among many bare patches of earth—the remains of a tribe. I followed my parents to our tent, where we sat silent for a while till my father asked my mother to make us tea.

In the afternoon I went to the spring where the animals used to drink at that time. There I found the few animals of some people from Dura. I saw the places of our tribe's sheep and cows. They were empty, some still keeping the hoofmarks of the animals while others had been swept clean by the wind. I passed also by the big pine tree where the shepherds used to sit at noon and sing or play games. I found just two shepherds sitting alone under the tree. They were eating their food as I came near. They asked me about the tribe and I told them.

In the evening we were called by my father, who began to make the coffee. 'Set the fire, and you,' my father said, 'get the *mihbash*.'

We all, except my mother who was busy on the other side of the tent, sat around the fire as the sun was setting. In front of the tent I could see the places of the tents—many trodden spots, with some blackened stones and some other trifles. I began to think where our people were now. I tried to take the *mihbash* and crush the coffee, but my father took it from my hand and began to beat. But it did not sound like my grandfather's beating. My father, perhaps feeling the same as me, began to adjust the rhythm, but it still did not sound as it should. My father's beats followed each other rapidly, as if he were trying to be done with the job as soon as he could. I served the coffee to my father and to my mother, who had joined us.

That night I felt a great loneliness. I felt as if I were completely alone. At first I was given courage by the moon, but soon it sank behind the mountain and it became completely dark outside. My young brothers slept deeply, but I was unable to sleep. I tried to speak with someone, but there was nobody. My mother had gone to bed too, and my father was in the men's part of the tent. I thought of many things, but they had no certain link. I tried to force myself to sleep, but I could not.

It was nearly midnight when I felt someone moving in the men's part. The movement began just after the east wind had begun to blow. We generally disliked that wind and did not feel easy with it, because it was not the one we were used to. The sound became louder and my fear increased. I was about to cry out, when the movement stopped. I tried shutting my eyes, but still I had the same fears. Long minutes later I heard some broken tunes sent up by the *rababa*. I tried to get up and see who was playing at that late time of the night, but I could not. The music became clearer and a little louder. It met the night. I think that it did not go far to the east because of the wind, but certainly it went further to the west, driven by the newly blowing wind.

As the sound got louder I raised myself and looked through a small hole in the curtain between the men's and women's part. There in the faint, undulating light I saw my father sitting, his face towards the west, and in his lap there was a *rababa* which I had not seen before. I had not heard my father play on any musical instrument. He had always been serious: and so he was that night, even though he was playing. He stopped playing, stirred the remains of the fire and began to heat his *rababa*. He was deeply pensive as he turned the instrument this way and that. Then he tightened the string, tested the instrument and began to sing.

It was a sad song, reflected on his thin face, which appeared strange to me in the dancing light of the lamp. I could not grasp all that he sang, but I felt that it was deeply sad and that it was about the self-torture of a man who refused to go with his people and followed another way. I still remember some of the lines :

> When will you return home,
> O men who went up the far mountains?
> I wish that I had not left you
> To stay here alone in the darkness.
> Return! Return! The hills are calling you.
> The dogs are wailing and the children crying.

The wind became stronger and the lamp was blown out. It became completely dark. At that moment my mother got up. I felt calmer and I got up, too, and went to the men's part where my father was still singing. He stopped for a while, then went on a few minutes after my mother also arrived. My mother lighted the lamp again, and we all sat around the dying fire. We sat silent, while my father began to sing in a low tone. Outside the tent and on the site of one of the removed tents, our dog stood wailing. My mother tried to stop him, but he moved to a far off spot and went on with his crying.

I did not sleep that night. In the morning my father went to the town and returned in a blue car in which we moved to Dura, the neighbouring village. But there were no people to bid us farewell.

# CHAPTER 12

# *In a Late Spring, Long Ago*

'DON'T forget to visit your aunt,' my mother said, as I was leaving. 'She is always asking about you.' I promised her to pay the visit.

I was going to visit Omar, who tried his luck outside Jordan, then returned to stay as one of many youths in Aroub, a refugee camp. After great toil he found a humble job, clerk in one of the Bethlehem restaurants. He was lucky, because many of the other young men did not find such opportunity.

It was not the first time I had gone there. The great numbers of small white tents were not strange to me—they were everywhere. I had been there in winter time and felt the great troubles that the family of Ali, the husband of my aunt, had faced as one of the families there.

Omar talked to me about the bad situation in the camp as we were walking along a crooked path to Ali's tent. When we reached there, Omar tried to return, but my cousin Wakid saw us and invited Omar to enter. Hearing the voice outside, Ali came out of the tent and welcomed us. Before we had entered the tent, the whole family was outside to meet us, except for Hoda, their young daughter, who stayed within to prepare the sitting-place.

Omar, despite being a stranger, was received as a relative. They forgot him as they began their family questions. I told them that I had met Ratib, their eldest son, who was working in Amman with one of the airline companies. I did not tell them that he was working as porter, and was content to tell them that he was living happily. It seemed to me that Ali knew about his son's job, for he did not enquire about that any more. The small children asked me many questions about big-brother Ratib, and I told them as much as I knew would please them.

I felt their need as Hoda was dealing with the three cups, two of which had broken handles. She blushed as she brought them on an old tray. Ali was the same as I had known him many years ago—smiling and kind to all those around him.

The time came for me to leave Omar and the camp and the various people now living inside it. As I went along the road winding among the green trees, I began to recall what I heard many years ago.

It was a sunny day at the end of spring, and the last days of spring time were hard ones for cow-herds. A very strange insect— the gadfly, I believe—usually appeared at that time of year and bit cows, causing a very great pain which made them run madly to try to get rid of that damnable insect. If a bitten, running cow came to a peaceful herd it would cause a great disturbance, with the whole herd spreading in all directions, leaving the poor cow-herd alone, unable to do anything but wait till afternoon, when that insect stopped biting. It was the more dangerous because cows used to damage the newly ripe fields of wheat, barley and lentils, which caused much trouble between the farmers and the cow-herds.

But cow-herds found a solution to that problem in our country. Deep gullies had been made by erosion, so cow-herds used to keep their cows in one of those gullies and sit at the only opening from which cows might get out.

It was one of these hard late-spring days when Ali missed one of his cows because of that insect. He did not leave his cattle until the afternoon, when he thought that the insect would not come again. His cow might return on her own if he left her, but he was afraid that she would go to the field of Salamah, a man who was ready to quarrel over the most trifling things. So he brought his cattle to a wide plain and asked Abdulla, one of his friends, to take care of them there until he came back.

Tired and anxious, he left. But even though these days were hard they had some kind of beauty. The weeds and grass were at the end of their days. Most of these plants were yellow and about to dry, except those which were in the beds of the small gullies caused by erosion. Few flowers could be seen. It was the time of ripeness. Everything was at the top and it was the season of fullness, fullness of anything being the beginning of its collapse.

Ali could see, very far from him, a very big *wadi*. He thought that he might find his cow there, so he followed a very narrow path leading in the direction of that *wadi*. From time to time he left the path to have a look at one small *wadi* or other, where he hoped to find his poor cow hiding in the shade.

Among the ripe fields he could see the heads of the storks. They were few, because most of them had already left for the places from where they had come. A month later one would not see any of those big white birds, because those that did not leave would die. At the beginning of spring they would fly up if anyone came near, but now they did not move as Ali passed near them. Ali could see also the fledglings of larks and other small birds, being taught flying by their mothers. He heard the drowsy buzzing of the different insects.

He could see all these things, but he could not that day feel their beauty. He felt melancholy, but he was unable to tell why. In all his nineteen years he had not felt such a feeling as he did that late spring day.

When he finally reached that big *wadi* he could not see anything, but he heard a low and soft voice: it was singing. He approached the place where the sound was coming from, and he knew that the sound was that of a girl. When he arrived he saw a girl, alone, with a black sheet on her head, sitting not far from her cows and sewing on another black piece of cloth. Before she became aware of the sound of his footsteps, he greeted her. As she turned her face he saw that it was small, heart-shaped, and of a delicate, melancholy beauty. She was surprised, and blushed a little.

He greeted her, then asked, 'Have you seen a black cow? It was bitten by the cursed gadfly and left the herd before noon.'

'No,' the girl answered, 'I have not. I have been here for three hours and I have not seen anything.'

Ali stood for a while. Then he said, 'Thank you', and left.

'She's not from our tribe. It's the first time that I've seen her. She is very beautiful. I must see her again,' he was murmuring to himself while he was leaving. He began blaming his cow for making him leave.

He found his cow about two hours before sunset and returned to Abdullah, whom he found sitting near their cattle with his sling in his hand, throwing stones at one of the big stones that stood as landmarks. 'So you've arrived at last! Come, let's see your skill at throwing stones,' Abdullah said. Ali was distracted, so he refused and sat near their small heap of belongings—two sticks, two small bags and two water-skins. Abdullah was unable to understand what was going on in his friend's mind, so he put it down to fatigue, from hunting for the cow, and went on alone with his game, shouting and praising or scorning himself according to the stone he threw.

Next morning Ali gathered his cows, met his friends and went to the same place where he had seen the girl the day before. But there was nothing. This was repeated for six days without his having seen that unknown girl and small, unknown herd.

On the seventh day he played a trick on Abdullah and told him that they were going to change their usual place: instead of going to the place they now agreed upon, he left for the customary spot. This was only a few miles from the deserted hills where it was said that ghosts of soldiers killed in the first war used to appear at night.

Those hills were at the borders of Ali's tribe, the Diqs, and the Almasharfah tribe. Among those hills there was a very big one, called Tel Al-Nijieleh, where it was said that the biggest cannon had been sited. Ali saw that big hill and thought that the singing girl must be from the Almasharfah tribe, because it was the nearest to his, and occasionally some of their shepherds came over our tribal borders and were welcomed by our cow-herds and shepherds. He thought of going to these hills and standing upon Tel Al-Nijieleh, so he might see that girl. Despite its being very late he ran quickly and drove his unfortunate cows with his stick to the south. There were some clouds in the sky and the harmful insect did not appear. He reached the hills one hour before sunset, because he had in fact to let his cows stop more than once to eat of the untouched grass.

He had been there twice before, but with other boys. He felt a kind of dreariness and loneliness. At the bottom of Tel Al-Nijieleh he saw some of the empty shell-cases and some spots where grass did not grow, so he believed what he had heard about the places where the grass did not grow because men had died there. Although he was nervous, he left his cows grazing happily and went up that big hill. When he reached the top he was able to see more and farther than ever before. He saw the land of his tribe, and knew all the places he saw and found them wider and more beautiful. When he looked to the south he saw Almasharfah places and, far away, their many big tents. Here and there he could see a few other tents, one here and two or three there. There were also many flocks of sheep and herds of cows, spread over the wide green plains and upon the small hills standing there. The sheep were newly shorn and they had been washed, so they appeared very white, as if they were new-born. All the cows seemed black and smaller than they were.

To the west of the tents he saw near a hill a number of cows, nearly the same in number as those which he had seen with the girl. He could not see the cow-herd: he saw a black heap among the cows, but he was unable to tell whether it was a calf or a person. He kept his eyes upon that small object, till it got up and he realized that it was, indeed, a cow-herd.

'She may be the girl I saw that day. Oh, the sun is sinking and she's getting ready to go home. Who can tell me where that girl came from?' He was talking to himself. He looked sadly at the girl who was driving her cows. Then he went down, gathered his own cows together, and went slowly behind them.

The next day he set off earlier, so he was able to go far beyond those deserted hills. He saw the unknown cows nearer than the day before. His poor cows missed a lot of the good grass they passed by, until they came near the place where the cattle of the day before were once again grazing. Then he left his cows to graze greedily, and went towards the others.

Not far from them he saw a girl working with a needle on a small piece of white cloth in her hands. Seeing him, she raised her head and looked at him. She was the girl. He blushed, but came near and addressed her.

'I am sorry for having disturbed you,' said Ali, 'but I came here to ask you about a drink of water.'

'I've no water with me,' she said, 'but there is the blue *gadeer* in that *wadi,* where you can find plenty of clean water. It seems to me that I've seen you before—aren't you the one who came by in the *wadi* a few days ago, on the western side of Wadi Al-Hisi?'

'Yes, I am, and it was the first time I saw you there. I think you're not from our tribe.'

'No, I'm from the Almasharfah, but that day most of my cows, driven by the fly, had run to where you saw me.'

Ali knew that it was not so good to stand and speak with a strange girl for a long time, so he left her after thanking her and telling her, indirectly, that he normally came daily to Tel Al-Nijieleh because there was a good place for cows to graze and a big *wadi* to keep them in, safe from the insect. As he left he wondered whether she would come to the place he had mentioned. It was between the two tribes and she might come.

When he reached the place the next day he did not see anyone there, but he left his cows and went up the hill and looked to the south. He looked towards the tents and saw that everything was as he had seen it before, but he could not see the girl in her place. He looked everywhere, but could not see her. He stayed on top of the hill for more than an hour with his face towards the south.

Turning back to his cows at last, he saw that they were more than usual. He looked carefully, and knew that strange cows were among them. He thought, at first, of his friend Abdullah having come after him, and was surprised when he saw the girl, a few yards off, coming up the hill towards him. He smiled and told her that he had expected her to come and was looking for her. She sat down a few feet from him.

He told her many things about his life, and how he kept on thinking of her since he saw her singing in the *wadi.* Naifa, for that was her name, told him that her father was dead and she had her mother looking after her two small sisters and young brother. She told him also that Rashid, one of her relatives, wanted to marry her, but that she did not love him. She was afraid because Rashid watched her always.

'He is lazy and always sitting in the *Shik,* depending upon his brothers,' Naifa said. 'I am ashamed to talk about my relative so, but these are the facts. He may come and see us, so I prefer to leave now.'

**111**

'But remember' said Ali, 'that I will come to Tel Al-Nijieleh daily, and that I'll be there waiting for Naifa to come.'

For many days afterwards one could see two groups of cattle on the usually deserted hills. All day they did not come near each other, but as the sun went down they drew nearer and nearer, till they became one after sunset and stayed thus for two hours, and sometimes more, in the darkness. The deserted hills were no longer fearful to the two young lovers. It was safe and quiet for them, because no shepherd or cow-herd was willing to visit that place after sunset.

The couple even began to doubt the rumours about the ghosts of the soldiers who had been killed—but that was only till they saw one night that their cows had stopped grazing, pricked their ears and begun to beat the ground with their hoofs. Naifa was very afraid, and for the first time she came close to Ali and caught him with her trembling hands. He could feel the beating of her heart and smell her sweet breath.

'It is a ghost : I saw him passing near that cow,' Naifa said in a shaking voice.

'But I don't see anything. Don't be afraid—you're just imagining,' Ali said in a tone full of manhood. But he had to accompany her that night to her tribe.

When they came up one of the hills on their way they could see the faint light of the small paraffin lamps in the unseen tents. They were silent as they went along the track, empty because all the cow-herds had already gone home. Before he left her he put her hands in his and asked her, 'Do you promise me?'

She did not reply for a while, then said in a very faint voice, 'Yes, I do,' and Ali felt a few warm tears fall upon his hand. They stood silent with their hands still together, while her cows were making their way home in the darkness. They did not stay like that for more than a very short time, because they heard far away, in the direction of the tents, the barking of dogs. Each went on his way, full of happy thoughts.

Ali found his own cows still grazing, unaware of what was going on in their friend's mind. He looked here and there, but did not see anything unusual. Because it was very late he rounded up his cows and followed them on their way home.

On his way he thought of his meeting with Naifa and how one

day he would marry her. But Rashid came to his mind. He would marry her, then, in spite of Rashid, since she had promised him. He imagined how the horsemen, boys, girls and women would go, following a decorated camel, to bring his love; and how everyone would try to show that his horse was better than the others; how the horsemen and the people of Naifa's tribe would meet them. It would be his happiest day. The women of both tribes would bring Naifa in a decorated howdah on that well-dressed camel. She would be carrying a sword in her hand, because that was the custom. He would pass her on his fleet white mare and perhaps she might smile to him. Then he thought of his small tent which must be built far from the tents for the marriage days. These thoughts were broken when he saw the lights of the tents and heard the dogs barking.

The next day he followed his cows and went to the same place, but in vain. He saw neither Naifa nor her cattle. He spent the whole day there, but no one came. He went up the highest hill and he saw the tents and the animals as he had seen them before. He waited till the evening, hoping that Naifa would come. The sun sank and it was night, but she did not come. He waited till it was late indeed. Then he left and followed his cows.

More than a month passed without meeting or seeing Naifa, but those long days increased his love and made him the more anxious to meet her. He thought of her being ill—but that would not happen suddenly and it would not last for long. His thoughts at last settled on Rashid trying to marry her. He thought of a way to learn about her. He had heard that there was a forthcoming marriage in the Almasharfah tribe, so he decided to persuade some of his friends, even though it was far, to go there at night, for young people used to go to other tribes in such cases. They used to sing all along the way till they came near, when they would be met by some young people from the other tribe, come to welcome them by answering their songs.

The next night some young bedouin men were passing by Tel Al-Nijieleh and breaking the night silence with love songs and with others about the strength and generosity of their tribe. Ali was with that group: he had been unwilling to sing, but was obliged to do so because it was he himself who had persuaded them to walk that long distance in the darkness. As they approached they raised their voices—many shots were heard and then they were met by a group of young men, of whom they knew some as cow-herds or shepherds whom they met from time to time in the fields. They were welcomed and led to the big tent where the people assembled many nights before the night of marriage.

It was a big tent with two lamps on each side and one lamp hung on a pole in front of the tent. There was a crowd of people, old men sitting on the right in front of the tent, and a long line of more than thirty young men in a row clapping their hands to the same time and dancing to the rhythm of these claps. In front of the line there were two men, one of whom chanted a line of bedouin singing verse, with the other answering him, while the whole group of dancing men repeated in turn each line as a chorus. It was a kind of chanted debate between these two men from two different tribes. Between these two men stood a woman in a full, long dress, dancing with a sword in her hand. No one could come near, because the well-respected tribal laws gave her the right to strike anyone who tried to touch her.

Inside the tent there were women : some of them were dancing and others looking at the dancing men. Children were everywhere : they destroyed the habitual division, but went inside and came outside the tent following whichever dance they thought best, and sometimes making their own dances or games. Tea, milk and coffee were being served all the time.

When the news spread among the Almasharfah tribe that some of the Diqses had come to join their happy nights, they were welcomed by the two dance leaders and by many special songs from the women inside the tent. Ali, with the other Diqs young men, joined the long line of dance soon after they arrived, but his thoughts stayed with Naifa. He could not see her inside the tent because it was a little dark and one outside could not distinguish women inside, but women within could see the men without.

After a time Ali felt someone touching him from behind. As he turned his face he saw a small girl beckoning him to follow her. His heart beat quickly, he released himself from the dance and followed the small girl in the darkness. She stopped and he stood by her side, anxious to hear what she had to say.

'The ghost is real, your friend told me, and she is forbidden to go out with the cows. She is keeping her promise. You must meet her near the "blue *gadeer*", where she told you once to drink. Remember, tomorrow two hours after sunset. She wants to tell you important things.'

The small girl said the last words while she was disappearing in the darkness. She did not give him the opportunity to ask any questions. In vain he tried to follow her, because soon she disappeared among the busy children.

He did not go back to dancing, but stood in the right-hand corner near the old men watching the dancers. Now he was unable to follow the story that the two men began to tell in their song.

On their way home his friends were happy although they were tired. Everyone began to give his impressions about that night and about some of the beautiful girls they had glimpsed inside the tent. After they exhausted their talks about the festivities, they began to sing some songs suitable for that late time of the night.

Ali was walking with them, but his thoughts were with the small and mysterious envoy and the one who had sent her. He tried to recollect exactly the words he had been told and to make an effective whole of them. It was clear to him : Rashid was the cause. He made up his mind to meet her at the place she had appointed. He knew the spot well. It was a pool where water was found the whole year through. The water was blue and clean. Shepherds used to tell that it was a bottomless *gadeer*, for they had never seen its bed. It was in a *wadi* about three yards deep, which led to Wadi Al-Hisi. There were a few plants on the edges of that *gadeer*. Some birds used to come to drink, and footprints of beasts were seen sometimes on its sandy edges. Young girls from the Almasharfah tribe came sometimes in daytime to get water, so as to find an opportunity for singing and for chattering about love affairs.

Ali could not sleep that night, because he was thinking of this unexpected meeting. The next morning he drove off his cows, followed by his mother's enquiring eyes.

He went to the eastern side of Tel Al-Nijieleh and spent a very long day. It was a day of waiting and suspense. He could see the *wadi* where the blue *gadeer* was found. He saw a few girls go to that *gadeer* in the afternoon. After sunset he heaped his cloak on

**115**

a stone where he had been sitting, to show his cows that he was still there, and left the herd and went to the Blue *Gadeer*.

He reached the place and found that it was silent. Nothing at all was to be heard. He stood there at the edge of the *wadi* for a while. He was looking towards the tents, but no one came. The small path was deserted. Then he called in a low voice, 'Naifa, Naifa. But no one answered.

He waited for more than an hour. Then he thought that something had happened and she was prevented from coming. He had to leave. But she might come : she was true. So he waited for more than another hour and then left because he knew that it was late. When he came to his cows he found them in their places, lying down and ruminating. He roused them and drove them home.

The next morning he went with his friend Abdullah to Tel Al-Nijieleh, where they found some of the Almasharfah cow-herds at its top. These told them the sad news of what had happened the night before. One of their very beautiful and well-behaved girls had been found dead in the Blue *Gadeer*.

'Her beautiful hair was floating on the surface of the blue water,' one of the cow-herds said, 'and her embroidered small piece of white cloth was at the edge of the pool. My old uncle, after looking carefully at the place, said that she might have been frightened by a shadow, perhaps even her own reflection in the water.'

'Poor Naifa—she was the best of our girls. No one now will drink from that damned *gadeer*,' another one added.

Since that time the name 'Blue *Gadeer*' was heard no more, and 'Naifa's *Gadeer*' took its place. And, indeed, none of us drank from it any more. And perhaps nobody drinks from it still.

# CHAPTER 13

# *Theban*

I HAD been far away from my family for two years, when one evening last August I returned from Saudi Arabia on leave. The taxi in which I came from Hebron could not reach the small house where we now live in Tarqomia. I got down my bags and paid the driver, who left directly. One of the students whom I once taught was near. He offered to help me carry the bags, and I accepted his offer because I wanted to appear suddenly to my parents and young brothers. In less than five minutes I was at the gate. I asked the boy not to make any noise, neither did he, but we were discovered by Theban, our dog, who was lying in a pleasantly damp spot behind the gate.

The dog got up suddenly and barked as he jumped to attack me. I was puzzled whether to keep silent or to call for the family inside, but the dog had hardly touched me when I shouted, and soon it stopped near me, waving its tail left and right and moving its head up and down. Hearing the noise made by the dog, Amal, the six-year-old daughter of Hassan, my brother, opened the door, stood silent for a while, then shouted, 'My uncle! My uncle!'

Instead of coming towards me, she went running and shouting, 'He has come—my uncle has come!'

Before I could get through the gate my father and mother came hastening towards me. As I embraced my father, he seemed to be many years older than when I had left him. My mother was weeping with joy as she kissed me. It was a happy meeting. They all sat round me in the shade of the northern wall on the concrete paving in front of the house, sometimes to ask me, and sometimes

117

to answer the questions which arose in my mind at that moment. My brother's two small daughters began to quarrel about who would sit closer to me.

In front of us Theban was still standing waving his tail and head, and looking towards me as if he were trying to recall my image to his mind. I called him by his name, and he increased the rate of his tail and head as he came nearer to me.

It was not the Theban whom I first knew. That was one of the sons of my grandfather's bitch. He and his sister, Samha, came to me as a gift when we were living happily in Wadi Al-Hisi. They were both of the same age and of nearly the same colour—brown on the back, a little white at the belly, and a little black at the head. They were of the ordinary type that bedouins used to keep for guarding their sheep by day and the camp by night.

I liked these two dogs very much and felt proud of them. It was unusual for one to get dogs for one's own in a family, but I kept on claiming that these were mine. Our family and the neighbours accepted that, and began to speak of them as my dogs. They were faithful and they used to follow me wherever I went. More than once I was blamed by my father, who kept on saying that I would spoil the dogs by pampering them.

'To get good dogs you must tie them,' he used to say.

I still remember how once, early in the morning, nearly at dawn, I went out of our tent. It was spring time. The grass was wet with dew. I was encouraged by the nice morning to follow our cow-herd, who was beyond the nearby hill. I was unaware of the two dogs which were following, till they passed by me, swift as the wind. I stared in the direction they went, to find out what they followed. They were hiding their tales between their legs and their stomachs were almost touching the ground. There was a white-tailed fox in front of them.

I followed them, running in the dewy grass so that I was soaked almost to the knees. I disturbed the birds which, awakened by the dogs, flew up, and then tried to alight, only to be forced to fly up again as I passed. Samha drew closer to the fox, but she could not catch it because it moved quickly both to the right and the left. They were about to catch it, when it jumped into a gully and I could see them no more.

I was tired, so I was panting as I ran slowly near the edge of the gully. At last I was unable to run more, so I sat on an elevation near the gully and began looking towards the north, the direction where the hunt was going on. A few minutes later the dogs came back, and they were panting as they sat in front of me on their rumps with stretched forelegs. I guessed that the fox had reached its hole before they could catch it.

The next summer I was sent to the boarding-school in Beer Al-Saba. The dogs were greatly missed, but at last they were forgotten in the new life I led in a boarding-school in a big town. They were the first to meet me when I returned home from the school, except for that last time when I was received by their mother, lonely with her young pups.

Theban was lost once when we were driven off by the Zionist tanks at night. I did not miss him during all the next day, because there were many other things to worry about: these included killed and wounded people  The next night I missed his voice among the barking dogs near the still dismantled tents. His sister was the second who seemed to be missing him too, because she spent that night sadly howling, and her wailing echoed between the two high mountains.

Two weeks passed and nothing was heard of Theban. It was foolishness to ask about a dog in such cases. In spite of feeling this, I asked those people who I felt were not mourning. No one could tell me anything about the lost dog. Every night we were reminded by the wailing bitch that had not slept all these nights. Some of the people were annoyed by her howling and spoke of it as a bad omen. This talk was repeated more than once, so I was asked more than once to silence her. She refused to stop crying, despite the stones I threw at her.

Feeling that she was unwanted near the tents, she used to go far away to the top of a neighbouring hill, sit on her haunches, and carry on calling for her lost brother. My father was annoyed, and I heard him say more than once that he would stop that evil dog for ever. I felt that he meant his words, so I asked him one day if I could go and look for Theban. Knowing my great love for the dog, he agreed, and told Hassan, my elder brother, to accompany me, because at that time I was suffering from a heart complaint.

Early in the morning we both mounted our white she-donkey

and went westwards  We felt that the best way to follow was that by which the tribe came.

'If it is still alive, it may be at one of the springs in this *wadi*,' my brother said, 'or do you think that it returned to the last place we were?'

'I feel that he is still alive, but I'm afraid we'll not find him,' I answered.

We passed by many of these springs and saw a lot of animals there. There were some dogs among them. At one of the springs I saw a similar dog lying in the shade of a rock near the spring, and I was about to call 'Theban', when the dog was awakened by a cow and I found that it was different. I was disappointed, but still I felt that we had to reach the last spring so as to use the last shot in our quiver. There we found some people whom we knew. When we asked them about the dog, we were told that a dog of the same description had been seen with Abu Rabba, who was now near a village a few miles from the place. In spite of its being late, I begged Hassan to go with me there. He kicked up the donkey so as to reach the spot well before sunset.

When we arrived there we kept on looking at the dogs, which barked and began to attack us. Theban was not with them. Although feeling that he was not anywhere there, we asked the people, so as to be sure. They told us that they had seen such a dog strolling near the neighbouring spring, but that was about a week earlier. I felt happy because now there was a possibility that the dog was alive. Feeling that it was too late and of no use to search more, we went home

When we came home we found that Samha had been given to a man in the small nearby village. I was very angry and I asked my mother how it had happened.

'Thank God that he did not shoot it,' my mother said. 'He was about to do so, but your brothers' weeping prevented him.'

I heard then that he had ordered our cow-herd to take the dog and get rid of it. The kind boy took it and, as he was going through the village, a man asked him to give him the bitch. He did so, willingly.

I went the next day to the village, then on to the place which the cow-herd had described to me. I found the poor dog tied by a chain. There was a circle round her, made by her trying to get rid of the chain. Seeing me, she stood up and began to wag her tail and jump up and down. I was thinking of setting her free, when a tall, fat man came out of the house and asked me in disgust, 'What are you doing here?'

I knew that I had no right to claim the dog, so I said, 'Nothing!' I left Samha trying hard to get rid of her chain.

Two weeks later I went with a group of young people to get water from Ongor Spring. It was a little far from the tribe, on the slope of a mountain whence its water descended down the hill among the huge walnut trees. On the slopes there were some terraces irrigated by the Ongor water. There was an old road passing by that spring. It had been prepared for asphalt and then neglected, so there were small stones in the road which made it difficult for animals to tread. Along the road, and about fifty yards on each side of the spring, there were two stone walls about one yard high. Near these walls, and under the shade of the trees, there were many animals—cows, sheep, a few donkeys and camels resting at noon. Upon the walls the shepherds were sitting eating their food or playing, and not far from them, at the end of the tree shadows, their dogs were lying.

We filled the tins and drums. Some of our animals left the spring slowly, because of their heavy burden and the protruding stones smoothed by the effects of time. I was helping a man, by supporting one container on his camel's side while he went round to put its twin on the other side, when I saw the dogs pass, running very fast towards the south. Turning towards them I saw their quarry—a brown dog with its tail between its legs and coming towards the spring.

'Leave the dogs, otherwise the water-can will be dropped,' the man said. After finishing the work I followed the dogs with my eyes. The brown, thin dog went to the side of the wall and began walking more slowly, but one of the dogs had already reached it and now began to attack it. The brown dog tried to defend itself, and it would have succeeded if the other four dogs had not backed the first one in its attack. Each bit the intruder from each side, while it went round in circles trying to keep itself away from their sharp teeth. But they came closer and closer. The poor dog was extremely confused, because I saw it twisting and leaping all ways. Feeling its weak position, it tried to flee. But it was too late, because the dogs attacked fiercely and threw it down. I felt that it would be the end of that dog.

Seeing the shepherds careless or unaware of what was taking place, I ran towards the fight, picking up stones as I ran. It was very difficult to separate them, because the poor dog was laid on its back under a huge black one. I caused some confusion among the attacking dogs, helped by some other boys who had perhaps come just to watch the battle. To my great surprise it was Theban, my dog. He was covered with blood as he fled when he got the chance, but the dogs followed him. I followed them, and threw my big stones at them fiercely. Theban was extremely exhausted and now was unable to run. He moved with desperate steps.

'Theban, *kis, kis*! Theban!'

Hearing my voice calling, the poor dog turned his face. He saw me and came towards me in spite of the dogs being in his way. He came and threw himself at my feet and smeared them with his blood.

I sat down and began to stroke his back. I felt it was useless to stay longer, and stood up and called Theban to follow me. Afraid of the other dogs, he walked in front of me.

On our way home I noticed that Theban was indeed very thin. He could not have eaten for a long time. As it seemed from the old wounds that covered many parts of his body, he had been attacked more than once by dogs as fierce as the ones I had seen a few minutes before.

'Don't you think that Theban has rabies?' Hassan said. 'Look at his tail pressed deep between his legs.'

'No, I don't think so. Because, if it were so, he would bite me,' I answered.

Before we reached the tribe Theban appeared to be better and his tail began little by little to rise. As he was walking he came more than once to rub his nose on my legs, and looked up at me with a very kind look.

One evening, a few days later, we were sitting in front of our tent. The sun was about to sink while we sat talking about the hard days we were passing through and about the unknown days to come. Our talk was interrupted by my brother Idris saying, 'That's Samha! Samha!'

We all turned our heads and I saw Samha walking slowly towards the tent. She walked, then stopped, as if she were afraid of being dismissed, but I ran to her, calling up Theban to follow me. I can still remember how their meeting went. They both began to sniff at each other, and to rub noses and heads with each other. When I returned I saw my father gazing towards the dogs, and he did not speak a word.

Samha stopped howling. She stopped eating and drinking, too. My mother threw her a loaf of bread : she smelled it and took a crumb, but I noticed how it was difficult for her to swallow it. She tried again, but failed to get the piece of bread down. Drinking was easier for her than eating. I asked the advice of Ahmad, an old man who was famous for curing animals. His advice was not encouraging, for he said that, if it could not swallow soft food and liquids, then there was little hope of recovery.

Ahmad's prophecy was right. Three days later Samha was found dead, near a stone not far from our tent. She was lying as she had slept for the past three years, but this time not to get up again.

The custom was to throw dead animals away far from the tribe so as to avoid the bad smell when they rotted, but I, helped by Hussein, our cowherd, made a small hole on the other slope of the mountain and laid Samha there forever.

We were followed by Theban as we were carrying the dead she-dog to her resting place. He stayed at the grave for a while— then followed us.

As long as we stayed in that place I used to pass by Samha's grave at least once a week. Theban did not howl, and I attributed that to his being a male and to the great troubles he had met when he was lost. He soon forgot Samha and began to appear as happy as any dog in the tribe. He began to perform solo guard duties and he became more active at night. One no sooner heard his barking on one side than one heard it again on the other

One night we missed our white donkey. We looked everywhere, because we were afraid that it might have been attacked by beasts. At last it was found by my father about two miles from the tribe, and, to his surprise, Theban was there, sitting on his rump a few yards from the donkey.

Three years passed. Then we shifted to Dura, a village not far from Hebron. There my father rented a small house of two rooms, with an open yard outside. In that house in the village two creatures stayed indoors like prisoners—my mother and Theban. My mother hinted at this once, when she was angry with Idris, my brother. 'It is just for your sake,' she said, 'that I have spent three years as if I were in prison, never going outside the house.'

I could not think how she spent those long days inside a small house, visited seldom by some neighbour-women who, when she did not return their visits, ceased to visit her. We were at school and my father used to visit some bedouins near the village. It was difficult for my mother to accompany him, because she was the only bedouin woman in the village, as she said.

My mother was able to express her complaints, but Theban could not. He spent two years and about six months just the same as my mother, though on the wall of the open yard. Being accustomed to barking at strangers, he used to follow any passing people along the top of the wall and bark at them. Despite his not biting anyone, some of the neighbours complained of the noise he made at night. So he was tied at night and released at daybreak. On Fridays I used to go with my brothers outside the village to spend a day in the countryside, and Theban used to follow us on that weekly trip.

Our house was on the main asphalted road of the village. The gate of the courtyard was about three yards from the road. When it was open, the men passing in the street could see inside the house, and so it was shut all the time except when one was entering or leaving the house My parents were always afraid that my youngest brother, Zakaria, might be run over by the cars which used to pass in front of the house, because he used to rush quickly from the gate into the road, and that was another reason for the gate to be locked all the time.

Years passed and I became a teacher, and took my share of the responsibility for my old parents and young brothers. I used to live in the same village where I worked, and not to come home except at the end of every month so as to give my father the twenty pounds, my salary. I enjoyed that kind of work, because I felt that I was doing something for my parents who had sacrificed themselves for us, and I felt prouder when I saw my brothers growing up and being top of their classes, except for young Zakaria who would spend all his free time playing with Theban.

At the end of one month in spring time, I returned home. I had some gifts for my brothers. When I reached the gate I was met by Zakaria, who began to kiss my clothes as he could not reach up to my face. I had hardly sat down, when he asked me, 'Where is Theban? Do you know what happened?'

'No. What's the matter?' I had really missed the dog, because he used to meet me before anyone outside the gate.

Zakaria tried to tell me what had happened. But, feeling that he could not give the exact details, my mother told me the story.

'Three days ago it was, nearly at noon. Your father was on his usual visit to Abu Tamaa who, as you know, is not far from here. I was alone at home, Theban sleeping in the sun as usual, inside the gate near the wall. Zakaria, as always, came from school a little before your brother. He entered and, it appears, forgot to shut the gate. He was asking what I had prepared for dinner when we heard a shot. It was very near, as if it were inside the house. Just at the same moment we heard a cry. Zakaria rushed out and cried, "Theban! Theban!" I followed the boy and there just near the door I saw Theban soaked with blood, creeping towards the door. He had barely reached the boy's feet, when he fell lifeless. Zakaria threw himself down and began to sob, trying to get Theban to move. But it was useless.

'I went to the gate and saw a policeman with a gun walking slowly along the road. I knew why he did that: he was patrolling as there were dogs with rabies in the district. When I returned, I missed Zakaria. I looked for him in the eastern room, but he was not there. As I came out the door to look for him in the other room, I saw him, splashed with blood. And your father's pistol was in his hand.

' "I must shoot him, the beast of a man!" he declared as he rushed for the gate. But I caught him before he could reach it, and kept him till your brothers came and the policeman had taken himself off to patrol elsewhere.'

# CHAPTER 14

## *Headmaster*

It was a Friday evening at the end of September 1954 when I left Nablis on my way to Tolkarm, a small town a few miles to the west of Nablis. The road passed through some small villages. They seemed to be better than the villages in the south, near Hebron. Olive trees covered all the mountains I passed. I could see the farmers returning from their groves, driving their animals, burdened with olives, down the slopes. The dress of both men and women was a little different from the southern villagers' dress. Near the road I saw some young men playing cards in the coffee shops. Some of these people looked at us in the bus, perhaps looking for a friend, then returned to their cards.

Two miles before we reached Tolkarm there was the Refugee Camp. It was almost sunset when I passed by the great number of small white tents which were arranged in rows. They were so close together that it was difficult to distinguish one from another. I do not know why I then remembered Japha, with its beautiful streets, green gardens and white sand when these people were living there.

The school was at the western side of Tolkarm, close to the border. After I reached the outside gate I went between two rows of high trees. There was no sign of movement on that road. At its end was a very green and well cut hedge. When I came to the start of that hedge I saw the school.

I had already formed a picture of the school as a great and huge building, but now it stood in front of me like an eagle—completely different from what I had imagined. It was exactly like a huge bird—two wings, a neck and a head. It was built of stone and its roofs were of red tiles. There were some old trees which went higher than the two-storeyed building. Two jasmines were at the main door of the school At both sides there were bougainvilleas hanging, with their red flowers. Here and there, under the few trees near the school, there were some old logs of wood, on which the students used to sit in their free time. Nearby there was a doorkeeper, who showed me in.

The life in the school was not new to me, because I had spent more than three years in the boarding-school at Beer Al-Saba. I found no difficulty in the life there, while many of my classmates kept on complaining of the life there for months. I knew that I had to spend three years there so as to get a diploma in agriculture, and thus it was the beginning of a long road. I felt that I had to work very hard in order to get outstanding results, because there was a rule that the one who got good results had to be excused from paying the thirty-five pounds of school fees for boarding and lodging. I began to work from the beginning.

The rules of the school were very strict. We were not allowed to go to the town, except once a week. That was on Fridays. We had to study one day in class and the following one in the field. I enjoyed that alternating system very much and used to await the field day anxiously, because it was really interesting. Boys used to be divided into groups, each one having to work in a different part of the large farm. Some of us had to work in the animals section, some in the nurseries, and others in the poultry section. I well remember how Jamiel, a foreman, made us do a tremendous job of work the first day in dividing the land into squares for alfalfa cultivation. I learnt afterwards that the school had a special machine for that task, but it used to be done manually on the starting day of every year so as to show the boys the kind of work they had chosen. It proved effective, because when we returned to the field on the third day I missed one of the boys : he had left the school, saying that he had not come to work as a labourer.

I had heard many things about Ali Raof, the headmaster. All the students used to respect and fear him. It was said (and it proved to be true) that, once he had decided, no one could ever persuade him to change his decision. In spite of its being a government school, he ruled the school in an entirely personal, centralized way. The Ministry of Education had great confidence in him. I still think that he was the best possible man to manage that school.

I did not see the headmaster until the third day, when he passed through the dining hall. I felt his coming by the sudden silence in the hall—even the sound of spoons and forks was heard no more. I turned my face a little and saw him—a bald, middle-aged man with a pipe in his mouth. His eyes showed a strong personality. In spite of being a little lame, he seemed to be active and strong as he walked between the two long tables in the long hall. He was wearing the same uniform dress as ours, khaki shirt and trousers. He did not speak, except for a few words to the teacher who was responsible for keeping order. Then he left the hall, and everything returned to its former state.

I liked the system which was followed in the school. I enjoyed both classes and field work, where we sometimes used to sit around Abu Zuhair, the fitter, listening to his oft-repeated tales. He used to behave as if he knew everything in life. Some of the naughty boys knew this weak point and began to ask him questions to which he answered in detail, and a long time was wasted. Then it seemed that Abu Zuhair began to abandon this practice. One day I was the fifth in a group which was sent to work under him. He seemed to be more serious than on any day before. He stood huge in his oily clothes near a tall palm. As we reached him, he distributed us. 'You and you go to this part and clean this side of the machine,' he said, 'and you both go the other side.'

I was left alone and was disappointed because he was not going to tell us tales. He stood watching how the work was going on. Then he said to me, 'Come and copy these papers. Take care that they are in a good, clean handwriting.'

I followed him to a small table with a small chair in the machine-room. Despite my trying to keep the papers clean, spots of oil got on to them. I sat on the chair and took out my pen and asked him, 'What shall I do?'

'Write from this page, and don't forget a single word, because every one has its meaning and importance.'

It seemed to me a better job than that of my friends, so without asking him another question I bent over the small table and started copying from the badly handwritten papers in front of me. Soon I became bored with these papers, and wished that I had taken my place with my fellows among the oily machines. Afterwards I learnt that the papers were a draft for a book which was being prepared for publication. It had been re-written more than once by the schoolboys who came before us, perhaps ten years previously. There were two or three chapters completed, and I think nothing has been added even now.

Abu Zuhair was completely different from the other instructors. They were diligent and serious in their work and we really benefited from their teaching. In spite of his not visiting them very much, they were well known by the headmaster, and he saw to it that, when the students were divided into groups, Abu Zuhair was given the smallest group.

I used to see the headmaster in the field more than in the classes. I had not seen him indoors except in his two classes weekly. He proved to be highly qualified and we understood his subject more than that of any other teacher. He passed hardly any point without giving a detailed explanation. He had a great confidence in the staff, but they used to avoid him. His room was always shut and nothing could be seen through the window, for it was covered by the jasmine.

In the south wing of the school he lived with his small family— his very old mother and old sister. Both his mother and sister were hardly seen. They spent all the time inside the house, except on the rare occasions when they used to walk in the very beautiful garden. It was said that no student had entered the headmaster's house, so it seemed as mysterious as a mountain-top monastery. It was the same as the north wing of the school, which we were allowed to visit when we liked as it was occupied by some of the teachers, but still we imagined that the south wing must have something different.

Once I entered its garden to do some pruning. I saw that the garden had many different kinds of flowers, shrubs and trees. They seemed healthy and well looked after. On one of the terraces I saw the headmaster's old mother. She was very old and her grey hair was neatly combed. She was stooping as she walked forward. I had heard that she was kind to the boys when she happened to meet any of them, but I could not believe this when

I thought of her son who was *feared* by all who knew him, even in the Ministry of Education.

'Good morning, boy,' she said.

'Good morning,' I answered.

'How long are you going to stay in the garden?'

'Till I finish my work and I think not before leaving for dinner.'

'I'll see you before leaving.'

Then she went inside one of the mysterious rooms. She had been very gentle as she talked to me in her very low voice. Remembering what I had heard from the people in the school about the headmaster not marrying, I began to wonder why he preferred to stay with the women of his family instead of getting married and having beautiful little children to play in this beautiful garden. He must be thinking of something else. I did not know why I began to compare him with Abu Zuhair, who had a lot of children and had not been serious except when he talked about his orange-farm which was not far from the school but in the occupied part of Palestine. I went on with these thoughts to the sound of my pruning-shears. I was roused by the old woman's voice calling me. She was carrying a tray in her shaky hands.

'Here's some tea and cakes,' she said. 'Sit down and have a cup of tea.'

I was about to refuse, afraid of the headmaster coming, but the old lady put the tray on the edge of the wall and sat on a nearby chair, and I had no choice. As I was drinking the tea I answered her enquiries about my mother, father and my small brothers. I felt a great trust in the small old woman, so I started telling her the whole story of my life—even the private details which had not been told to anyone before in the same way I told them to that old woman. Was it because I wanted to know the intimacies of their life as I told her mine, or was there any other reason? Anyhow, I had confidence in that old woman.

When I finished my tea, I thanked her and left the garden. I went out by their garden-gate and she was still sitting on her old chair.

Two years passed, in which I knew the school better. I realized why Kadori boys were proud of their school. It taught manhood morals as well as scientific theories in agriculture. We used even to feel a special dignity when we heard the boys of other schools in the town calling us 'ploughmen' or 'the rough people'. Ali Raof, headmaster, was one of the most important elements in our pride. We feared him, but still outside the school walls we liked him and were proud of him. I think that he had the same feeling towards us.

It seemed certain he liked us. Once we went on a trip to the east bank of Jordan. We knew nothing about his people, all that we knew was his small family of old mother and sister, but on that trip we learnt more about his people. They were living in Al-Adassia, a very beautiful village. It was surrounded by banana plants and citrus trees. It was spring time when we visited that village. There were a few families scattered in among the green trees. Every house had a garden full of roses, jasmine and other flowers.

We were led to the guest palace. I could not believe that such a small village could have such a grand palace—indeed, have a palace at all. We found that everything had been arranged for our visit. The supper was an excellent one. The amusements which were prepared filled our night. It was a moonlit night and we were all happy. We began to dance and sing, and were joined by the teachers and the people of the village. Abu Zuhair danced and sang, too. The headmaster did not appear while we were singing, and we knew that he realized that we would not have done anything if he had been present. The next morning we left, and I wished that I could have stayed longer in that village.

A few days after our return from that trip, we missed the headmaster for three days. Then we were told by some of the teachers that he had a dangerous fever.

'The doctors are puzzled by his fever,' Nussaiba, one of the teachers, said. 'He has been unconscious for the last five hours.'

'I can't believe he is ill,' said Arafa, one of the school jesters, 'Ali Raof is stronger than illness.'

Despite Arafa's comments we suggested that we had to visit him. Since it was impracticable for us to go as a group, we decided that we would send six representatives from the three classes, two from each class. I was one of these representatives. We took a bunch of orange-blossom and went to visit our headmaster.

It was evening when we rang the bell of the outside door. The door was opened by the headmaster's sister. We introduced ourselves and told her that we wanted to visit the headmaster. She let us in to the eastern hall, where there was no one except a dreaming white cat, and we entered. There was a thick Persian carpet and leather pouffes.

On the wall there were very strange pictures, of which I could understand nothing. To me they were just a mixture of colours done without any care. I said to myself, 'They are like the scribbles done by my youngest brother.' On the opposite side I saw a picture of a young lady with a small boy and a girl a little younger than the boy. The mother was looking at both of the children with a very kind, motherly look. Soon the headmaster's sister came and beckoned us to follow her. This we did.

Then we were in the headmaster's bedroom. He was lying in his white bed with his eyes closed and his healthy face was pale and thin. On a small chair, his mother was sitting near his head. He did not feel our coming. We stood silent, as the boy who was carrying the orange-blossom gave the flowers to the mother, who took them and brought them near the man's nose as if she were trying to get him to smell these flowers grown by him.

'These are your boys, my son, they have come to visit you,' she said. 'Talk to them and tell them that you will go back to them.'

The man seemed to hear what the old woman said, but he was unable to answer. He opened his eyes. They had not the glitter they had had before. No word was spoken at first. Then I saw him collecting his strength as if he were going to say something. He whispered, 'Thank you, my boys,' and he was silent again. Some tears made their way down his cheek and settled near his nose.

'It is the first time for two days he has spoken,' the mother said.

We left the place and found a crowd of boys waiting for us outside. We had to give an account of our visit. Some of the enquiries were about the headmaster, while most of them were about the household—the mother, the sister, and the house which had never been entered before.

Two weeks passed and Arafa's prophecy proved to be right.

The headmaster recovered. Again he was frequently seen in the field and seldom in the classes, but now he stood, talked with us, and sometimes joked.

In July of that year I graduated from the school with outstanding results. I had reached a position where I was able to take on my responsibility in the family. The graduates had not to make applications for posts: the headmaster used to arrange for that. So I decided to spend a happy vacation after a long time of studying.

One day, in that summer, I was walking with a friend in a street in one of Jerusalem's suburbs, when I saw a car stop and a hand wave towards us. 'That's the headmaster's Consul,' said my friend.

'But what is he doing here?' I asked. 'And why has he stopped?'

Then I went over to the car on the other side of the street. It was the headmaster. He got out of the car and shook hands with me.

'Have you made any applications for work?'

'No, I haven't, Sir,' I answered.

'I have recommended you for a post in the Centre for Scientific Research in Dair Ala. Go there and see their conditions.'

'Thank you, Sir. I'll go tomorrow, and I'll tell you next day what has happened.'

'I shall not be at school the day after tomorrow.'

Without thinking I asked him, 'Where will you be then?'

The headmaster smiled, and said, 'I shall be on my honeymoon.'

# CHAPTER 15

# *A Young Voice Remarking*

In a flat of three rooms in the main street of Riyadh I now live with five friends. Rents are very high compared with our salaries. We have found it better to live together and save money for our families left behind.

I persuaded my friends to give me the room with the balcony. The room was empty when I arrived, and I had to get it furnished. A bed, an old table, two chairs and a clothes locker bought from the second-hand furniture market were the only things I had. Seeing my books scattered on the table, a kind friend offered to make some shelves to put them on, and so he made three book-shelves which were considered to be an important new thing in the flat for about two days. As I was working in agriculture, I was able to bring five pots: I planted a carnation in one, an asparagus-fern in another, and three 'morning-flowers' in the rest. These flower pots stand on the broad edge of the balcony.

The other rooms are not too different from mine. In the hall there are five old red-velvet-covered armchairs. Against the wall, not far from the door, there is the big armchair. These old armchairs were bought from the second-hand market, too. Being so big they seemed to be odd when first bought, but then they became an important part of our flat decoration.

In these armchairs we sit when we have free time, sometimes playing cards or dice, sometimes listening to Yosef's long-drawn-out stories, and on a few occasions listening to Abu Hamed's strange ideas about life. He lives in a village ninety miles from Riyadh, but he comes to visit his brother, who is one of the flat-dwellers. In spite of their being strange, we still feel that his ideas are real. We lead him on to speak about marriage, of which he talks in detail. We like that man to visit us, but not to stay long, because when he comes to our flat many people come—to greet him, perhaps to hear his arguments, or because they really want to see him.

Many of the young people are attracted by his talk, and consider him a walking encyclopaedia. One of these I will here call Hatim.

Hatim, then, studied with me at Beer Al-Saba, but I did not see him again till we met in Riyadh. He visits us at home, but not much. Despite having lived for a long time in town and being highly educated, he still keeps on speaking in the bedouin dialect, which gives his speech a certain effect. Hatim is married and he has a small child.

One night I was alone in my room, reading (or, rather, still reading) *Crime and Punishment*. Abu Hamed was reading too, outside in the hall. He was sitting in the biggest armchair. There was no one from the group in the flat, all of them were outside : some were working, while the others were sauntering in the streets. The bell rang, and Abu Hamed answered the door. I would have preferred to stay with this infinitely long book I was reading, but my old friend did not let me alone. He called, 'Here is Hatim. Come and let's have a talk together.'

I had no choice, so I left the book in my room and joined them in the hall. I was not interested in the company, but I had at least to listen. Each admired the other, and when one talked the other listened attentively. Abu Hamed's admiration was based on Hatim's goodheartedness and good character, so he said, but Hatim admired Abu Hamed as an intelligent and deeply thinking man. On this occasion I was struck by the proportion of Abu Hamed's silence. He was trying to get Hatim to do most of the talking by asking him questions, which the latter answered only too willingly.

Abu Hamed's questions concentrated upon love and marriage, and he began to give examples and explanations. Hatim was pondering.

'But no one,' Hatim said, 'can deny the importance of love. It should come before marriage, but it is not necessary that every love story must end with marriage.'

'Love first, then possess,' Abu Hamed said.

Sometimes one feels that one has to tell something that one suffers from, for then one feels a release. This was the case with Hatim when he began to tell his story. He began speaking like one possessed, who had found an opportunity to get rid of the things boiling inside him.

'Ria is her name,' Hatim (as we are calling him) said. 'She was nineteen years old, one year older than me the year we were driven out, the year of war. All of you must have passed through those dark, bloody days. In those days I forgot about Ria and felt that even to think of such things was a nasty thing. We settled in a refugee camp in the southern part of Gaza. Feeling some chance of continuity, people began to look for their relatives. Few of our relatives came in that direction, for most of them had left for the east and stayed in a camp near Jericho.' Hatim stopped for a moment to adjust himself in the armchair.

'It was the first festival outside our country. In accordance with our customs in such cases, my father wanted to go to my aunts to greet them, and to give them and their children some presents. But as he was alone in the tent he decided to stay, and—because I became a man then—he told me to take the few gifts and represent him. Really he was glad to see his eldest son becoming a man and able to take on responsibility.

'I was glad, even proud of doing this job. Early in the morning I put on the best clothes I had—they were not new as they should be, but still they were the best. Then I took up the presents and my father's apologies and went to the camp where my aunts were staying—one with her husband, and the second only with her children, because her husband had already been killed in the war.

'Most of the people in that camp were from El-Majdel, which, as you should know, is one of the industrial towns in Palestine and famous for making a good kind of cotton cloth, especially that used for women's dresses. There in the camp I saw the women and children treating the festival as an ordinary day—no songs, no dances and races.

'My aunts were more pleased with my visit than with the

136

presents I brought. Their children sat around me and began to ask me a lot of questions. While we were drinking the tea—and to my great surprise—Ria's father entered the tent. It really was a surprise, because I was not expecting to see him, for I thought he had left with our people for the east. As I saw him I remembered Ria, Ria the girl whom once I loved.

' "I'm very glad to see you," I said to the man. "Where are you living now?"

' "In this camp," the man said.

'I thought of Ria living not far from us and how I should be happy then. I thought of a way to make the man shift from this camp to the camp we were living in.

' "The people—there, in our camp—mention you often, especially my father. He wishes that you were with us."

'It seemed to me that the man was not satisfied with his circumstances, because he accepted the proposal and said, "I will take the opinion of my wife and my daughter." I was quite sure of Ria's word, but uncertain of her mother's. The man insisted on my going with him to have a cup of coffee. I accepted the invitation and followed him at once.

'Ria and her mother met us outside the tent. She seemed to be more beautiful than the last time I had seen her. She blushed as we shook hands with each other. Perhaps her mother had noticed that, because she was smiling when my eyes met hers.

'Before we finished the coffee-drinking the decision had already been taken, and the day was appointed. I bade them farewell, and I still remember how Ria stayed for a long time outside the tent, till I disappeared from her among the many small white tents.

'When I returned home I told my father about my meeting Abu Ria, and hinted that he would come to live with us. Then I told them the day fixed for Abu Ria's coming. It did not seem strange to them and they attributed the move to the new life in the camps.

'Ria's family came and they were formally invited, about four times, by the people who were living there. I felt happy because Ria was so near. I was told then by Ria that her mother knew that I loved her, so their tent was the safest place for our meeting.

'At school I was one of the best students and my father had

received many congratulations from the headmaster. The term that Ria's family came, I began to do worse in class. When the term ended and grades appeared, I had failed in two subjects— history and geography. The headmaster was surprised to see my results, so he called me to his room. "Why has this happened this term?" the headmaster said. "Have you any excuse for your result?"

'I tried to find an answer, but I failed. The headmaster, perhaps, was expecting me to apologize and to promise that I would do better, but he was disappointed. Seeing me standing silent in front of him, he became angry and said, "Get out, dirty boy! Don't come without your father."

'My only course was to obey, so I went out quickly, trying to avoid the outcome of his anger, which might be a slap on the face or a blow from the stick which was on the table in front of him. On my way home I thought of a trick to satisfy my father, who was waiting for my school report. He was expecting congratulations, but I brought neither the report nor the congratulations.

'There were three men sitting with him in the tent when I came in. Perhaps he was talking with them about my being the top of the class, because as I entered he said, "Here he comes." He turned to me and added, "Why have you come so early, Hatim?"

'I hesitated at first and waited for a while without saying anything, then remembered that I could not return to the school unless I had him with me. So I said, "The headmaster has dismissed me from school because I'm not as well dressed as the other boys. He told me to bring you, so as to get you to buy new clothes for me."

'My father turned to the three men and said, "Tell me if his clothes are different from other boys?"

' "No," the man sitting next to him said, "his clothes are better than my son's.'

' "I must go to the school now, and see what he means by that.'

'I accompanied my father to the school. As we reached the headmaster's room I waited outside. My father knocked on the door and entered. Being ignorant of the real reason for my dismissal, he began talking loudly. There was a misunderstanding.

So the headmaster spoke loudly, too, because he felt that he was being insulted.

' "I've come here just to tell you that Hatim will not enter your school again," I heard my father saying to the headmaster.

' "He's no longer worthy of staying in my school!"

'Slamming the door behind him, my father came out of the room. "Follow me, Hatim," he said as he passed me.

'I followed him. I had not expected that the situation would be so bad. My plan was not to confront my father with the truth, but to delay it till he met the headmaster. Things had not gone as I planned. I was wondering where he would send me. He seemed to be thinking the same, because he was silent as we went along the road.

' "Tomorrow," my father said, "I will take you to Gaza College. There you must stay. It is a better school, with better teachers. You will be able to come home on Fridays." '

The flat's doorbell rang and two of the flat's inhabitants came. Hatim stopped narrating, to return their greetings and to light a cigarette which I gave him.

As he took his first puffs I remembered well what it was to 'come home on Fridays'. When Hatim went off to Gaza, the phrase would have meant nothing to me: I was still a boy in the tents, going to school in the neighbouring village, walking to and fro daily with my small brothers, spending every night at home. I suppose it was three years after Hatim went to Gaza that I went to boarding-school, that I learnt what it was to live in a school, in a town, and to come home not even on Fridays, but just once at the end of each term.

'Go on, Hatim,' Abu Hamed said. Hatim seemed to be in no need of encouragement, because he went on at once, even as the two newcomers seated themselves one on each side of him.

'For me this was the last thing to expect, and the worst thing at the same time. It meant that I would not be able to see Ria except on Fridays. I began to think of another plan. Had I to tell my father the truth? Even if I told him the whole naughty thing, he would not return to the headmaster after what had happened and he would be more angry. I decided that it would be better to go to Gaza College—and so I did.

'My father was expecting me to do better at the new school. He

139

was old, and as I was his eldest son he built much hope on me to carry the responsibility. I must be educated, then find a good job and help him with the family's responsibility. These were his hopes and they, in his opinion, justified his paying more money to send me to this college. I knew that he had not much money, and the little money he had would soon finish. I felt the necessity of working hard. Gaza College used to send monthly reports to fathers, telling them about their sons' results. In the first month my father received a good report.

'It did not last for long, because I began to find excuses for leaving the college and going home to see Ria. I gave false answers to my parents, saying that we had a holiday every time I came. My father seemed to suspect something, for he started making more enquiries when I returned home. He began watching me when I was at home, and once he asked about me and the answer came readily from my young brother: "He is in Abu Ria's tent."

'One day, when I was at home, my father received a note from the college telling him about my frequent absences. I was talking with Ria in their tent, when my young brother came and told me that my father wanted to see me. I felt the danger, because all the time I was expecting that something would happen and my bad tricks would be discovered. As I reached him, my father threw the note at me and told me to read it. I could not lie any more. It was true and I could not deny it.

' "I have met the headmaster," my father said, "and he told me the real reason for calling me. It was not your clothes, but your failure in two subjects. Now you are deceiving me again with your lies. Don't you know that I borrow money to pay for your education? You are a man and you must be true."

'I could not stay till he finished his speech, so I left for the college. I decided not to return again. I was extremely affected by imagining my father asking people to lend him money for my sake.

'I did not go home for a month, and decided not to go till the end of term. I made a noticeable progress at the college. I became glad of the good results I obtained. I began to dream of my happy future: the time I would get my certificate, find a good job, help my father, then marry Ria and live happily together. I began

140

recalling how often she had encouraged me to work hard and get the highest grades so as to be proud of me. It was only about a year till I could leave the college to work.

'At the end of the term I was top of my class. I was longing to return home and prove to my father that I had changed. On my way home I was thinking of my meeting with my father, and with Ria too. She might have heard some words spoken by my father against me and those who had led me to be lazy and a liar. I was sure that she was sensitive and intelligent. But now I thought that she would be proud, and perhaps would come to congratulate my mother in the presence of my father.

'My father was very glad when I delivered him the paper. All the family were glad, too. They began asking me questions about life in the school. I was expecting them to ask me about my absence for such a long time, but they did not, perhaps ordered not to by my father.

'I felt a great longing to see Ria, but I tried to hide my emotions. I could not wait. I was about to stand up and go to see Ria, when my brother, the young one, himself whispered in my ear, "Ria has left with her family for Jericho—a very far town, as father says." '

# CHAPTER 16

# *The World Advancing*

It was one evening in autumn a few years ago when a green pickup truck was leaving Riyadh towards the west. In the back there were many chemicals—powders in sacks and pots, and liquids in bottles and tins. In one corner there was a green motor-sprayer. There was a very strong smell: when that car went by, one would know that it was different from the great number of pick-ups which followed that asphalted road.

On both sides of the vehicle there were inscriptions denoting that it was owned by the Ministry of Agriculture. Four men were in the light truck: Awadh was the agricultural adviser, Fahad the driver, Muhsin a trained labourer, and myself a technical assistant to Awadh. We were sent from the agricultural directorate in Riyadh to two of the neighbouring villages, Muzahmia and Ghot-Ghot. We had to advise the farmers by showing them the best methods in cultivation and at the same time to spray the plants that had any disease or harmful insects. We had to stay there for a month.

It was nearly sunset when we were at Dirab, a twisty part of the road. It was the first time that I went that way, so I wondered how much great toil had gone into building this wide, comfortable road on such a rocky mountain. I looked at Fahad, who was twirling the steering-wheel while still joking at Muhsin, who was sitting near him. It seemed to me that Fahad was accustomed to that part of the road.

It was my first week on this job, so Awadh spent most of the time explaining to me the conditions of work. He was a good and highly qualified man, but he liked very much to talk. Muhsin avoided arguing with him in our free time, but Fahad like to tease him by taking the opposite side in every argument. We covered the distance, which was some forty miles, in about an hour.

We reached Muzahmia, the village where we had decided to live for the month. As we came near, I saw the dark-green palm trees on both sides of the road and I could hear the sound of pumping engines. When we entered the village I saw that Fahad was driving as if he knew the house in which we were going to stay. There were a few men passing along the sandy streets. Few shops were open. The people in those shops or passing along the streets looked at us for a while, as if to identify the newcomers. Some of the children, perhaps knowing the car by the words on its sides or by the smell sent out by the poisonous chemicals, shouted, 'Agriculture car! Agriculture men.' It seemed to me that the people there were familiar with groups sent by the ministry.

Soon our vehicle stopped in front of a house. Near the house there was a small shop. Seeing us, the shopkeeper came out and stood examining us. Before he could say anything, Fahad shouted, 'Hullo, Abdu. Have you the key? Bring it quickly.' Before Fahad reached him the man went back into his shop and returned with a key in his hand. Fahad hurriedly took it and opened the door.

Inside the house I noticed that an agricultural team had lived there before, because I saw some torn cartons bearing the ministry stamp. We began to get down our equipment: Muhsin worked most of all, while Fahad worked the least. He was talking and joking all the time. Muhsin, carrying one big box and trying to get it inside, stumbled and fell down with the box. I ran and carried it with Fahad, who did not stop laughing.

'Haven't I told you that you have become an old man?' Fahad said to Muhsin, who was still leaning against the wall, near the right-hand side of the door. Muhsin looked at Fahad, but did not say anything. When we came back to carry more things, Muhsin was still there in his place. We asked him if he felt any pain, to which he answered that he did not.

Soon everything had been moved into the house and we all sat drinking the good tea which was made by Muhsin. We talked about many things, especially our work programme. Awadh discussed this subject in detail. Perhaps he wanted to show me, as his assistant, how the work should go when perfectly performed,

**143**

because the next day I noticed that we could not in fact follow the programme exactly.

The next day, nearly at dawn, I heard a little noise. When I looked up I saw Muhsin passing near the window, then I heard him praying. He was reciting his prayers with some grammatical mistakes, but solemnly nevertheless. Fahad, perhaps awakened by Muhsin's praying, got up from his bed, washed and then went to pray. He carried out his praying more quickly than Muhsin, just as in everything else he did. Breakfast was early, prepared by Muhsin, helped a little by Fahad. Then we all left the house in our green car, apart from Muhsin who stayed at home to prepare our food.

I discovered later that Fahad, the driver, because of his long experience of these expeditions, had become as clever as Muhsin, so he worked instead of him on such occasions. In any agricultural demonstration he was ready to take the spade or the shears and do the required thing well. Later, when I used to go out alone with him, he used to tell me how some of the trained agriculturists were put in difficulty by the questions of some of the cleverer farmers. His talk about agriculture showed me that he knew something about agriculture, but not very much.

We visited some of the farmers on their farms. They seemed to be more interested in the insecticides and pest-control than in our expert advice. They had felt the prompt advantage of our chemicals. I noticed that Awadh had friends among them. They respected him, and it seemed to me that they believed in most of his advice.

We returned that day after doing a good job. Some of the farmers we visited insisted on giving us vegetables and fruit. In spite of our refusal, we found a small box of tomatoes and another one full of cucumbers in the back of the pick-up when we reached it. It was noon and we were very hungry. As we entered the house we were met by the strong smell of Muhsin's cooking.

'Hullo, my friend!' cried Fahad. 'What has the old man prepared for our lunch?'

'Are you hungry, baby?' Muhsin replied from inside.

I followed Fahad to the kitchen. There I saw Muhsin making salads. I asked him if he needed any help, but he said that it would be better if we left and went to wash ourselves free of the dust of the chemicals.

It was really a good meal. I wondered at first whether it was really good or if it seemed so to me because I was hungry, but later it proved that Muhsin was in fact a good cook as well as a trained labourer. He said few words in reply to Awadh's and my praise. Fahad praised him, too, but in his own funny way.

In the afternoon I sat with Awadh to write out some reports about the things we had done. While we were at our work I could hear some of Muhsin's and Fahad's talk in the kitchen. When we finished I went to see them and found that Fahad was washing the dishes while Muhsin was helping him.

'Today I passed a group of old men sitting near a wall,' Fahad said. 'I 'm quite sure they were talking about their old days. They made a very good sight, but there was something missing.'

'What was that?' I asked.

'It was Muhsin, whose place should have been in the middle, on the right of the grey-bearded old man. He would have talked to them about his golden days.'

'To be old is different from feeling old,' Muhsin remarked. 'I don't have that feeling.'

'Then why did you fall yesterday with the big carton?'

Muhsin was silent for a while. Then he looked from Fahad to me and said, 'Perhaps it was a stumble.'

Awadh joined us and he took Muhsin's side against Fahad. Then we left the kitchen. Soon Muhsin brought the tea. After drinking our tea we returned to do our afternoon work. We stayed working with the farmers till sunset: then we returned home.

In the evening we were visited by some of the farmers and some of the teachers in the village. These knew that we were in the village because we had passed by them in the morning while they were at morning gymnastics in front of the school. We talked for a while, then played cards. Muhsin did not stay all the time, for he went to bed early.

It was a Thursday night, our week-end, when we left the village at about eight o'clock for a place twelve miles to the west of the village, where we had heard that there were hares. I myself was fond of shooting, and so was Muhsin. Awadh was not clever at shooting, so did not join us. Neither did Fahad. It was dark when we left the village in a village car. Two villagers were sitting in front, while Muhsin and I stood in the back, whose canopy we had removed. I had the only single-barrelled shotgun at the ready, leaning on the roof of the cab.

I asked Muhsin about his family, and he began to tell me in detail about them, especially about Ibrahim and Abdul Razak, his sons. Both of them were at school. He told me about his plans to get them educated.

'Ibrahim wants to be a pilot,' Muhsin said. 'He has many models of jets and rockets at home. His mother doesn't want him to be a pilot, but to be a doctor as his brother intends to be. But I encourage him, and I feel that he will succeed.'

We were busy with our talk when suddenly we heard the horn of the car and heard Saad, one of the villagers, shouting, 'There's the hare—be ready!' We looked down the path of the headlights. I could not see anything at first, because it was the first time for me to go shooting at night. Then I saw the running, terrified hare.

Her ears were laid back, taut. She was trying to get out of the light, but was forced to return into the field of light because she feared the shadows of the small bushes, which seemed to be moving as the light of the car was moving. It was my first time to shoot hares at night and I was afraid I would miss. But my friends shouted at me to shoot, so I had no choice.

I missed her with the first shot, but killed her with the second. The car stopped and we got down to pick up our first kill.

'You have to shoot faster,' Saad said.

'And you haven't to confuse him by shouting,' Muhsin remarked.

We went on. The driver seemed to be experienced at following hares. He went to the foot of the hills, where there were small bushes.

'These are the usual places for hares,' Muhsin said. 'They hide all day in the shade of the small rocks or under the small bushes. They can't bear the sun's heat. When it becomes a little cooler at night they go down to eat—one or two hours after sunset till some time early in the morning, depending on how hot it is. The best time for shooting hares is when the moon has disappeared. The car's light can puzzle them and they can't see the car from a long way off.'

'There's one !' I shouted. Muhsin hammered on the roof of the cab, over the driver's head.

'Where is it ?' the driver yelled.

'To the right—to the right,' I shouted.

He seemed not to see her at first, but later the car went fast in a straight line after the hare. When she came within gun-range I shot : she fell wounded. But, when Muhsin got down to fetch her as the car stopped, the hare felt Muhsin's steps and threw herself into a desperate run.

I shouted at Muhsin to leave her, so that I could shoot her again, but he refused to do so and followed her. He chased her for about five minutes, then at last he caught her—but he was completely exhausted. He sat panting, with his hand on the left side of his chest. He dragged himself to the car, but he could not keep himself upright.

'Do you feel much pain, Muhsin?' I asked. 'If it's severe, let's go back to the doctor.'

'No, don't bother about it,' he said. 'It's not necessary. It's only heart disease.'

Three years passed. I was transferred to another job, in another place. Once I returned from my vacation and decided to see my old friends in the Ministry of Agriculture. They were very good and kind people. Even Awadh, who had been a bit troublesome, was good-hearted. I found that the best way to see them all together was to visit them in their office. So I went there.

I found everything more or less the same as I had left it five months before. I sat on a chair near Awadh, who began to tell me about their hard work as if it were new to me. He spoke to me about their new experiments, their nurseries and demonstration plots. Fahad, seeing me as he passed along the corridor, came to greet me. He was the same as when we had parted—laughing and joking, and arguing with Awadh when he found an opportunity to do so.

'Where is our old friend?' I asked.

'He's in hospital,' Fahad answered.

I was sad to hear that about Muhsin, the good man. I knew

that Awadh had been kind to him. He helped him very much. He had gone with him to many doctors. I knew that Awadh would know more about him.

And Awadh did. He told me about the floor and the room's number.

In the afternoon I went to the hospital where Muhsin was. I ascended in the lift to the right floor and then went to Room Two. But Muhsin was not there. I realised that I must have been given the wrong number, so I went to the nurse's office in that section. There I was lucky to find Abdu, a friend of mine, as the nurse on duty.

'Who are you looking for?' he asked, after we had exchanged greetings.

I told him. Then he led me to Room Five. While we were walking along the clean corridor he told me that Muhsin was in a dangerous state.

'Your friend is fighting a losing battle,' Abdu said. 'It is just a matter of months.'

When I entered I saw Muhsin on a bed. It was the only one in the room. He seemed to be surprised to see me. He tried to get up to greet me, but I hurried and shook hands with him before he could raise himself from the pillow.

In the room there was a gas cylinder. It was for oxygen, to help Muhsin in breathing. I understood that it was difficult for him to breathe, so he had been advised by the doctors to make use of that oxygen at particularly difficult times. In the room there were three other people : one was middle-aged, while the others were still young. One of these young boys insisted that I had to sit in his place. He then stood leaning on the bed's foot-rails at Muhsin's feet.

We talked about many things. He recalled some of the strange things which we had met in our time together. Then he talked about his son Ibrahim's success. The boy who was standing leaning on the bed blushed. I guessed that he was Ibrahim, and it proved to be true, for his father introduced him and his elder brother.

Muhsin asked me about my new job and whether I had got married or not. I answered all his questions frankly. I had an urge to tell him anything he asked, except the one thing which Abdu had told me a few minutes before.

The five of us had a good talk. We went in some detail into the future careers of the sons. The old man in the bed was eager to point out to me some advantages in the particular choices that I had perhaps overlooked.

When I was about to leave I saw, still folded, clearly of no importance there, a newspaper on the small table near Muhsin's head. There was printed in bold, red type and as the flaring main headline: MAN SOON TO LAND ON MOON.

I left the room. Along the corridor, as I went quietly back, treading the long, rubber-tiled floor, I recalled the few words once said in the darkness of the desert: 'It's only heart disease.'

# CHAPTER 17

# The Course of Events

Two years ago, in the summer, I returned from a visit to my eldest brother, Ibrahim. He was living with a group of our tribe at El-Kora, a few miles to the south of Madaba. El-Kora is one of the small villages scattered near Madaba. The people of these villages get their needs from Madaba, this being the central town.

I had not to stay for a long time, so I got up early one day and said goodbye to my brother. His children asked me to stay longer with them, but I told them I could not and promised to come again. They followed us as I went with their father, who insisted on going with me to the bus station. It is not a station in the real meaning of the word : it is just a place under a big tree by which the bus passes. If there are any people it will stop, and if there are none it will continue its daily trip uninterrupted.

We all sat down under the tree. My brother obliged me to sit on the stone which was near the trunk of the tree, while he and his two small sons sat near me. We began to talk about different subjects—past and future. The children listened at first to our speech, then, perhaps being bored, they forgot us and ran after a small grasshopper with red inner wings, which they were about to catch when it flew off and left them laughing. I do not know exactly how long our waiting lasted before the bus came.

When the children saw the bus they gave up the pursuit and came running towards us, to reach us as the bus stopped. I kissed them and, before I could step up into the bus, the younger one said, 'Don't forget to come soon and bring me the bicycle you promised.' As I turned round to answer him, his elder brother was

150

smiling as he said, 'No, he won't come before next summer. Mother told me.'

I could not say anything, because the bus had already moved off and I could only wave to them. I looked from the window as the bus went far away, and saw my brother walking home followed by his elder son, while the younger one still stood near the tree with his hands at his forehead, shading his eyes from the sun. The bus went down a hill and I could not see my small nephew any more.

The bus was full of people—men, women and some children. As the bus went on, new people came in till it could not take any more. But now and then the driver was forced to stop to pick up a friend, or a woman waiting alone by the road. Many people were standing in the gangway between the two rows of seats. The bus was old. I heard that it had worked for many years inside the town; then, being worn-out, it was sent to the outside roads. Every so often the vehicle was brought to a halt for the conductor to get down and pour water into its radiator from a container standing near the door. As we went on the stops increased. There were many people along the road who waved at the driver, but he would not pick up anyone, and when he was forced to stop he avoided the places where people were waiting.

The water finished before we could cover half of the way. There was no water and it was difficult to go on. Near the road there was a group of tents. When the driver saw them, he pulled up near an old man who was waiting at the roadside. As the door was opened the old man rushed in, but the conductor drove him back and left for the tents with the water-drum in his hand.

The driver got down and told the old man that they had no room and the car might not reach Madaba because of the lack of water. The old man followed the conductor. The dogs barked and ran at the conductor, who stood still, unable to go forward, and began defending himself against the attacks of the dogs. A young woman came out of one of the tents, but before she could get to him the old man had reached the conductor, driven the dogs off and taken the water-container from him. The young woman took the drum from the old man and then came back, walking heavily, and gave the water to the conductor. The conductor returned alone, while the old man went inside one of the tents.

Before the bus started, the driver blew his horn twice and told the conductor to call the old man, who accepted the invitation.

When the man got in I thought that I had seen him before. His features were not strange to me, nor was his way of speaking. I and another young man offered the old man one of our seats. He refused at first, but, when pressed, he accepted. Because it was nearer to him, the old man chose my seat, so I sat on the drum near the door, facing him. The old man gazed at me for a while, then said, 'Where are you from, boy?'

Feeling that he would in any case eventually discover who I was, I began, for amusement, by answering in a roundabout way. After getting only a little information, he guessed my father's name.

'How do you know my father's name?' I asked.

'Your features are the same as his. As soon as you spoke to me I thought of your father, but I thought that it is strange to see you here.'

I told Abu Sabah, as I knew him later to be, the reason of my coming there, and asked him to tell me about his life in that part of the country. The man felt that a common place in a bus was not suitable for a man to expose his private life, so he answered my questions abruptly and in a low voice.

'How do you think a man who is far away from his country is living?' The old man did not wait to hear my reply, but added in a louder voice, 'Nothing but poverty, debts, diseases and instability.'

The conductor interrupted our talk by coming to punch the tickets, but when he had passed I told the old man that it was the same for all of us and that he was no worse-off than all of us. Abu Sabah seemed to have found an opportunity to get rid of his troubles by telling some of them to me, so he went on: 'Today I am going to visit my daughter, who is seriously ill in the hospital, and to bring some wheat for the family if the tradesman agrees.'

I was about to ask him why he was coming alone to visit his daughter. But his ragged clothes, unshaven chin, and the tone in which he spoke about the wheat for the family—all this prevented me from asking.

As we were leaving the bus, Abu Sabah shook hands with me

and asked me fervently to carry his regards and good wishes to my father. 'Tell him, boy, that you met Abu Sabah, his partner in the horses.'

Then the old man left me. I followed him with my eyes through the crowded street. He looked at the shops as he passed them, even stopped sometimes in front of them, but I did not see him buy anything. I stood in my place in the open station till Abu Sabah disappeared in the long, crowded street. Then I left for the bus which goes to Amman.

Along the way from Madaba to Amman the wide plains in some places were covered with maize plants and water-melon. Some of the maize fields had been reaped, while the others had crops still standing, bowed under their heavy, white cobs. There were people—men and women—harvesting. The men were reaping with their sickles, while the women, who were fewer, went behind them, balancing on their heads the big baskets into which the men tossed the cut grain. I remembered how we used to do so when once we had fields to plant, and how the men used to sing and women answer their songs.

There were special songs to be sung only at maize-reaping time. Those men I passed might be singing the same songs, but I could not hear them because of the noise of the bus.

In the water-melon fields there were heaps of ripe melon waiting for buyers. In the middle of some of these fields there were sheds made of wooden poles with a roof of maize stalks. In these sheds there were people guarding the fields—an old man, perhaps, thinking of the profit he might get from his field, or a young girl knitting—and in some of the sheds there were children playing.

At other places near the road I saw some of the threshing-floors, where there were lazy people who had not yet finished threshing. On some of them there were machines doing the job, but on the others there were teams of oxen, donkeys or mules circling around and pulling the heavy, metal-bladed threshing-sledges, which we used to enjoy riding on when we were children, beating the poor animals to make them go faster. And I remembered how in the afternoon I used to go with my friends to let the animals drink, and sometimes to have races.

I reached Amman and went straight to the bus station where I

153

could get the bus for home. It was a long distance. The man who was sitting next to me leant on the bar at the back of the seat in front and fell asleep as soon as we got out of the town. I was left alone and this gave me a good opportunity to go far in my dreams. Many pictures came to my mind, some of the future and some of the past. But there was one picture which did not depart from my mind: it was that of Abu Sabah. At this time I thought of something that had taken place many years before, and of which I had heard tell more than once.

It was one day early in the autumn, when a number of tents stood on a broad, newly-reaped plain. The people of these tents had finished their summer-work—reaping and threshing the corn. It had been a hard job: people had to get up early in the morning, nearly at dawn, to reap. They could not rest except for one hour after sunrise, when all the reapers used to gather round their breakfast, which would have followed them into the field. Breakfast used to be eaten near one of the big corn-stacks where the water-container was kept. In the afternoon the harvesters would go home, where they had their dinner and took their rest till the next morning.

It was a good year, and the huge heaps of corn-stalks on the threshing-floor not far from the tents were true evidence of this. There were two golden heaps of wheat, perhaps the last of the year, and near one of them was a middle-aged man taking corn from the golden heap with a small cylindrical wooden pot and pouring it into a sack with two red lines held open by two young children. They were a small boy in white and his sister in black.

Near them was a young man, about twenty years old, adjusting the full sacks. He seemed to be active and healthy, because he was easily moving those heavy sacks. Not far from him there was a middle-aged woman busy closing the sacks with a big, shining needle and a jute thread.

The middle-aged man was counting. He did not follow the normal numbers, especially number seven which he skipped in the counting, believing that God would thus bless the harvest. Every now and then one of the children left the sack to be held by his partner alone and ran to drive off one of the small lambs attacking the other big golden heap. When the action was repeated often enough for the work to be interrupted, the man put down the measure full of wheat and shouted: 'Hoda! Oh, Hoda!' A young girl came out of one the tents and waved with her hand, but did not speak. The man with the measure called to her, 'Send Salem to keep these animals away. Tell him to be quick!'

The girl went back inside the tent, and soon afterwards a small boy, a little younger than the girl who was holding the sack open, came out running, with the edge of his dress in his mouth. He seemed to be customarily on that job, because as soon as the young lambs saw him they ran far away from the heap and went to the other part of the threshing-floor.

Near the threshing-floor there was a big tree. Under that big tree there was a young black mare with a blaze. She was tethered, and in front of her was a tub full of barley. She was not eating. She seemed to have eaten enough, because sometimes she kicked the pot with her youthful hoofs. It was clear that she was still more or less unbroken: she had no saddle nor its marks, and also she was no more than three years old. As the group worked, she was kicking the ground or the tub, and most of the time moving the flies from her soft skin with a swishing tail. Probably it was the young man's mare, because when he came to move the tub she began to rub her head on his breast, and when he left she made to follow him.

The number of the sacks increased, but the heap was almost as big as if it had not been touched. The man put down his measure and went to help the young man and the woman who was closing the sacks. His stubbled chin was covered with wheat dust, and on his clothes there were lines of sweat mixed with the dust.

Closing the sacks soon finished and he called the young man to him. Putting the youth's hand in his rough one, and leaning one of the sacks on their arms, he called the woman to help them, and she tipped the sack back while the two men lifted it up and then carried it to the two-roomed building nearby. One of the doors was open and by this they entered, to lay the sack gently near the high-heaped rows of other sacks. Then they returned for another. The two children, now free, were playing on the heap, while the young one taking care of the lambs was imitating his father in measuring and counted in a lisping tone.

More than half of the sacks were removed before the young

man felt tired and the sack began leaning towards his side. The youth did not complain, till all at once he was extremely tired and his hand slipped from his father's. His mother tried to help him, but the sack had already fallen to the ground just at the door of the granary. The father smiled as he looked towards his blushing son, then towards his wife, and said, 'You have kept on telling me to get Ahmad married. Don't you see that he is still young?'

The mother laughed. Trying to support her point, she said, 'But weren't you married when you were younger than Ahmad? And don't forget that Ahmad isn't used to such work. He was not taught to carry sacks at school.'

'You always find excuses for your causes,' the man said to his wife, as he held one of the full sacks as if he were testing its weight. Then he added, 'Come with your son and put this sack on my back.'

Before they could comment he had already squatted in front of the sack. The mother and her son helped him to get up with the sack on his back. When the children saw their father carrying the sack and running with quick little steps towards the granary, they ran after him, laughing. The small boy tried to help his father by pushing at the back of the sack, but his mother forbade him, because she was afraid that the sack might fall from the father's back and harm the small boy. This small boy then called his young sister and brother and tried to imitate his father unseen by the busy people, but before he could do anything he was discovered by his father, who ordered him to leave the sack alone and to help his mother and brother.

The sacks were all stacked in the granary and the whole family left for home. The dinner had been already prepared by the elder daughters who stayed at home. They all ate with great appetite, except the youngest child, who left them more than once to stop one of the naughty lambs which was trying to go back to the threshing-floor. At last his father told him to leave the lambs until he finished his dinner. To the child's good fortune all of the lambs stayed quiet, except for the very naughty one with brown face and feet.

'Leave it, Salem!' the father said, as he saw his son jumping up to get hold of it. 'A few days and it will be killed at your brother Ahmad's marriage.' The small boys turned happily to their elder brother and began to rub their hands joyfully.

156

'When will we begin singing and dancing, father?' the other small boy asked. Before the father could swallow his food, Salem and his sister repeated their brother's question, each in his different way.

'It isn't far-off. Just as soon as we finish our work on the threshing-floor. Your uncles and the other people will have finished their work, too, at that time.' The father then turned to Ahmad. 'Isn't that so, Ahmad? First we have to finish our work—otherwise rain will come and spoil everything.'

'Yes, father—as you like,' said the blushing boy.

It was Abu Sabah's family. Ahmad was the eldest son. He had left school recently, to help his father in cultivating the wide land and looking after their two big herds of cows and sheep. They had a shepherd and a cow-herd, and on occasions some labourers. But the presence of a keen young son was necessary.

This marriage had been mostly encouraged by the mother, who felt that soon she would lose her daughter, engaged to one of the best young men in the tribe. She would be happy to see her son become a man and married: in addition, his wife would replace her helpful daughter. So the mother was trying to get everything done as soon as possible, though with the luxury appropriate to Abu Sabah's respected family. When she returned from the threshing-floor she used to sit with her daughter doing the marriage preparations. The elder daughter was happy, too, for she felt that the same things would be done for her very near marriage.

The father, perhaps, was a shade less happy. He had been dreaming that Ahmad would finish his studies and become a doctor and have his clinic in the neighbouring village. He still remembered how once he read in the boy's composition copybook how his son wished to be a doctor. Since then he had thought of his son as a famous doctor in Al-Faloja, the neighbouring village visited by all the bedouins roundabout. But his hopes had soon disappeared, because the boy could not find a place in the secondary school in Jerusalem, so was forced to come back and stay with his family. It was difficult for Ahmad to do the hard work his father and relatives were accustomed to doing, but he had no choice. Abu Sabah felt that it was necessary for a boy of Ahmad's age to get married. There were no problems about marriage, especially for one educated and well-mannered like Ahmad. So there was no difficulty for Ahmad in finding the suitable girl.

Ahmad, as any boy of his age, was happy at his marriage. Sometimes he used to sit and think deeply. He had told no one about his life in the village school. Perhaps he had a girl there, perhaps he was just thinking of the great hopes he had when he was a boy at school. As he had been at school, so he was with the tribe—silent and polite. He could not compete with the other young bedouins in their games, but he could ride as well as his cousin Salem, who was of his age. That was why his father had brought him that young black mare with the blaze under the tree.

The filly was the daughter of the Kbiesheh, our own horse. Ahmad's father had not bought her, because it was unusual, almost deplorable, to sell good horses, especially females. He had taken her while she was still a foal, on condition that he had to bring back the first two of her daughters to my father, as was the custom. He had no right to sell the mare, nor to work her in any way. It would be shameful for him, too, to neglect her.

Ahmad loved the Kbiesheh, as he insisted on calling her. He was scolded more than once by his father because he was pampering the horse. He began training that year. He used to take her out when he was free, for a long time, and not return until sunset. When any of his younger brothers wanted to annoy him they just hit his Kbiesheh, or threw a stone at her. He hoped that he would be able to ride her at his marriage. He had heard many tales about her dam and wanted her to be like her. But his father kept saying that she was still young.

The small children also were happy at their brother's marriage. They worried about nothing in marriage, except to be sure that they would enjoy the songs and the dances of the young men. These dances and songs would last for about a month. They would not go to the other children's tents, but the others would come to theirs. They would enjoy the racing on the wedding day and on the day on which the bride would be brought from her father's tent. That was why they kept on asking their father when the marriage would take place : they did not mean the marriage, but its festivities.

All the family were happy in their own ways about that

marriage, and so were the other people of the tribe. It would be a high-point in their full life. As usual, all of them would take part in the marriage. There were no special invitations, except for the marriage preparations and the songs and dances which were held at night a month earlier. The dances and songs being at night would give the shepherds and cow-herds a good opportunity to take part with the other people of the tribe. They would not miss anything, as they would have done if the festivities had been in the daytime, when they were far beyond the hills looking after the animals.

The days went by and the preparations began. On the first night few people came. Most of them were children and young people from Abu Sabah's relations. The next night the number became greater and the people were older. The young people of the other tribes, perhaps hearing the news from shepherds, joined the dances. They were well received by the people in Abu Sabah's tribe.

Ahmad's family lost themselves in the nightly gathered crowd, except for their second son, the one at school, who began by looking on at the celebrations from a distance. He received the guests, his schoolmates, and then stood aside with them to watch and comment. But after three or four nights they all deserted their formality and took part in the dances, since the bridegroom had been one of themselves not a long time before. Abu Sabah's small children forgot about everything and wholeheartedly joined the other children in games. But they were interrupted by their father calling them to serve tea or coffee or to bring something needed on these busy nights. More than once their short line near the dancing men was broken by the father's or the mother's call. But soon it was filled by another boy inserting himself in the empty place, and the dance went on.

On the last two nights the number of the people was the greatest. They knew that these were the last opportunities, so the number increased. Ahmad was seen everywhere. He was happy, but he did not dance, because he was busy—except when his friends insisted that he should. Then he proved to be a good dancer despite the few occasions he had to dance. His father on the last three nights sang more than at any time earlier, and challenged his son to debate with him in song. Ahmad refused, among the laughs of his friends : he knew that he was not equal to his father.

The day came when the girl was brought from her family's tribe, which was not far away. There were many people. Because the distance was not great, women were on foot, while most of the men were on horses. The bride was on a decorated camel. On either side of her was a beautiful girl. Sometimes the bridesmaids took part in the singing, but most of the time they talked to the bride, who was sitting silent among them, high on her white camel. Ahmad was with the group, on his young black mare. He was surrounded by many other horsemen, and his father was galloping on his white horse all the time.

The group reached the Abu Sabah tents and the bride was led to the appointed tent, which was a little isolated from the others. The racing began. There were horsemen from nearly all the neighbouring tribes. That day was one of the occasions on which one horse might rise and another might fall. And the racing on such days was recognized, because many people would witness it.

As the women were singing and dancing and horsemen were racing, people began to come from the other tribes and offer lambs as wedding presents. Some of these lambs were slaughtered, to be offered as a dinner for the whole people. The women, too, gave the bride some presents. Among these presents there were pieces of gold, rings and necklaces.

It was almost two hours before sunset when the racing came to a serious point. Men of the different tribes were preparing themselves for that hour. They lined up in a long, expectant line. Ahmad came to his father, who was sitting with the guests in the big tent specially built for this occasion. Abu Sabah knew that his son's mare was still young and could not really compete with these well-known horses. but he could not refuse his son's plea.

All the people—men, women, children and even the bride—began to watch the restive horses. There was no particular man to give the signal, because as soon as they lined up any one of the riders could shout the beginning word, 'Go!' There was no man at the end, either, to tell the result, because the riders themselves would tell it and there had been no trouble about it before. The distance was great enough to produce clear results.

In the line there were some ten horses. Each man knew his own horse and the others, so he judged for himself whether to take part in the racing or not. At last the word was heard from more than one throat and the horses were off in a rush as the songs and shouts mixed together. All the people stood up to watch. There was a tree behind which the horsemen would pass, and then would return, but not by the same way.

In the first moments all the horses were close to each other and one could not distinguish which was ahead. Before the riders could reach the tree Ahmad's black mare had Ahmad's mother, his bride and most of the women shouting loudly for Ahmad, for she had already left all the horses behind her. Abu Sabah was standing, watching, as the others, but he did not turn to his youngest son when he looked up at him and said, 'Father, father! It's our mare, the Kbiesheh, in front, far ahead of the others. Ahmad is the first—look, father!'

The father was watching with all the people when the Kbiesheh reached the curve at the tree. There she turned, but she had thrown Ahmad in taking the turn. There was silence before people started running towards the fallen man. The Kbiesheh stopped directly and returned to Ahmad, stood near him before any one of the rushing horses could tread on him.

Most of the riders passed him, because they could not stop their horses. Ahmad was protected by the young Kbiesheh, not allowed to be trodden by the other horses. But she did not know that her friend had already died.

I heard that the young Kbiesheh was sent back with her dam, which did not take part in Ahmad's marriage but came, ridden by my father, the next day to follow him to his grave. My father did not reject the horse, in spite of considering that thing a bad omen. It was in the evening when my father returned with the other horsemen, but with a young mare running loose alongside.

I cannot remember those days, but I, as one of the children, was told by my aunt that the young Kbiesheh was regarded as an unloved animal. No one rode her, and no one gave her food, except my father who took a special care of her. She became familiar with my father and our tent, and began to come and go alone, as her mother did. Many people advised my father to sell her, though not one of them asked to buy her. But my father refused to sell and was seconded by Haj Ibrahim, my grand-father. They were satisfied to say, 'It is God's wish, and this animal is innocent.'

The forty days of mourning passed. It was nearly two hours before sunset. There were a few drops of rain, not enough to obliterate the tracks of two horses leaving our tribe. One was white, with an ordinary horseman, while the other was black, with only a very young rider. It was a father fetching back the Kbiesheh, ridden by his eldest son, though not now his first-born.

# CHAPTER 18

# *A Small Man Going Downhill*

At the end of the summer of 1959 I was transferred to Samo, a small village to the south of Hebron, to work as a teacher of agriculture in the only boys' school there. I think that it is a good idea having an agricultural specialist in every Jordanian village to work in its school. This man has to work both in the school as a teacher and in the village as an adviser. Most of the village schools have farms where the agricultural teachers can demonstrate modern methods. These kinds of teachers are obliged to live in the same village they work in, because in this case they have more opportunity of close contact with the villagers. A very few of those teachers were really willing to live in the village, while the majority accepted the situation just because they might not find better jobs. Because of my bedouin upbringing, I was of the former class, so it was not a surprise for me to receive the letter of transfer.

In spite of not having been to Samo before, I was glad, because I had heard more than once about the hunting mountains there where one could spend interesting week-ends. On the other hand I heard a lot about the school-master as a strict, rough, cunning man. I had not yet seen him, so I based my opinion on what they said about his appearance and character. Although I was happy in Tarqomia, the first village I worked in, I waited eagerly for the first day of October, the beginning of the academic year.

October is the month of real autumn in the Middle East countries, especially in Palestine, Jordan and Syria. It is a gift from nature to have four different seasons. The elements of nature suffer from declining life at this part of the year, but in

October the schools begin their year, so aspects of death and life are seen together—yellow leaves driven by the strong east wind and young, healthy boys and girls making their way along the roads in groups to school. The last days of September are usually busy ones for fathers preparing their sons for school after a vacation of a full three months.

I got up early in the morning and took my way towards the village bus station. Although it was early, the streets were full of life—small children carrying their bags and walking in groups, happy and proud of their new clothes, while others were crowded together looking at someone's new bag or someone's new magic painting box. I can still remember a small child who was puzzled, whether to hold up his oversized trousers or to keep his hand on his pocket containing five shillings, the fees for the school. Still that small boy was walking and, as others, looking both to the right and the left. Here and there I saw men hand-in-hand with their small children leading them to school, while women went their way towards the girls' school accompanied by their small girls in their new and clean uniforms. The elder boys and girls were not seen as much as the little children who did not know the exact time for classes to begin and who, because of the novelty of the day, went early to school. Along my way to the bus station I saw many of the secondary boys and girls who also were going towards the bus on their way to Hebron, where there were many secondary schools. One could sense the difference in appearance between these boys and those who were still in the village, not only because they were a little older but also they were smarter and better-looking.

The bus was hooting loudly as I approached to remind the secondary boys and girls that it was the time to leave. Some of the boys ran, while others walked slowly because they were accustomed to that horn and knew that it would not leave before six. It was a Mercedes, green, with two broad red lines along the sides below window-level. It replaced an old one, but it kept the same colours. The name of the village was written in big letters both on the back and the front of the bus.

It was parked beside a special low wall with steps to facilitate putting cases and boxes on its roof. In front of the bus Awad, the *mukhtar's* son, who was working as a driver, was leaning against the right front wheel. I greeted him as I passed and climbed in. All the seats were full of boys and girls. Most of the girls were sitting together, except for a few who sat beside their brothers or close relations. They seemed shy and modest. Few workmen were in the bus on their way to their work in the town. I saw no empty seat when I entered, but, before I could choose my standing point, some of the boys, whom I had once taught, stood up and invited me to take one of their places. I refused at first, but because of their insistence I sat in the nearest seat.

The bus moved off, and the noise of the boys increased. They were talking about different subjects, of which study was the main one. The girls were silent, apart from a few who were talking in whispers. Mahmoud, the conductor, began to do his job among the jokes of the boys. He was good and kind to them, and they liked him. But his goodness and kindness did not save him from their sharp tongues. He answered them back and they accepted his remarks with laughs. The bus picked up more boys and girls on the way and they joined their fellows in their endless talking. We went along the winding, narrow, asphalted road, through the small wood of green pine trees. We overtook some buses full of students from the neighbouring villages.

We reached Hebron, and most of the boys and girls got down before we arrived at the bus station. As I dismounted I saw, once more, streets full of boys and girls on their way to school. The boys were more active and the girls were less shy. One could easily recognize the village students because these walked in little communities.

The teachers going out to work in the villages were standing in groups waiting for the buses to come. They were in new suits, as I was too. As teachers we felt our importance on such days, but a few days later our standing in groups waiting for the buses to come would be an ordinary thing like any of our daily jobs.

I knew many of them and I wanted to greet them, but since I had no time I hastened to the bay for the Samo bus and joined that small group of standing teachers, who welcomed me as a new colleague. Not far from them were four girls whom I guessed to be the girl teachers. Soon after my arrival there came a fat, middle-aged man with a red face, bespectacled, wearing a head-cloth and head-rope, and with an old case in his hand. I knew that he was the headmaster. He shook hands with all the teachers, and I was introduced by a young and handsome teacher, who said loudly: 'Here is our new friend, the teacher of agriculture.'

Abu Alez, the headmaster, lifted the cloth from his ears as he saw the young teacher was talking. Then he smiled a childish smile and turned his face towards me.

'You are welcome to our school and we hope that you will enjoy your time in the village. We have a very nice garden, which needs green fingers.' We all laughed at his last remark. I felt that he had been misrepresented by the people who had talked to me about him. He seemed not to be rough as they had said.

Minutes later the bus came. As was to be expected, boys and girls got down. Some of them came to greet the teachers by whom they had been taught one or two years previously, while others passed quickly along the street and joined the long lines of students. The headmaster took his place on the seat just behind the driver, while the other teachers scattered in the empty vehicle. The girl teachers sat on two seats on the right. There were no people with us in the bus, except for two painters and a carpenter, because it was not the time for the villagers' return, which would be in the afternoon.

On the road we passed by the yellow-leaved vines, and I saw some farmers sauntering in the tomato-fields, while others were at the road beside their boxes waiting for the special trucks to load their fruit for Hebron. We passed by Yatta, a village not far from Samo. Then we followed the asphalted road between two close mountains, which soon led to an open plain where I saw Samo scattered on a small hill at the end of that plain. The bus stopped a few hundred yards before we reached the village. 'This is the school,' my friend said, as we were getting down.

We went through a large gate and along a small path between two rows of high trees. The boys were crowding on both sides of the way. Some of the elder ones came and greeted us, while the others were content to look at their teachers from a short distance off. The school was about one hundred yards from the road. It was built of white stone and surrounded by different trees. The garden was at the front. We passed up a few steps before we entered the school. Just at the main entrance there was the staff room and beyond it was the headmaster's office. Soon the bell rang and the classes began. I realized then why the people called Abu Alez a strict man. Everything had been already prepared and every teacher went straight to his class.

In the afternoon we had a rest of ninety minutes, so Abu Alez then asked me to go round with him and become acquainted with the garden, the farm and the other surroundings. 'Let us begin with the garden, if you don't mind? I'm interested in flowers.'

'And I am, too,' I remarked as we entered the small garden that the school had. There were different kinds of flowers, but carnations predominated. The carnation is my favourite flower, so I was pleased when I saw that the garden had it in many colours. A few rose-bushes, jasmine and, indeed, many other flowers were in the garden. Before we left it, the headmaster called for Shukri, the man who worked the garden. Shukri came. He was a short, plump man, wearing a blue shirt and trousers. Abu Alez introduced me to him : 'This is the new teacher. He is in charge and you have to obey him.'

Shukri welcomed me and followed us as we went to the poultry side. There were hens and rabbits. As Shukri opened one of the hen-houses, they came quickly round him hoping for food. Shukri looked at us and smiled. Then we left for the rabbits, which were kept in a small, half-roofed building. The headmaster began to explain, but often he was interrupted by Shukri, who at all times was ready with the exact information. It seemed to me that the headmaster himself had a great confidence in Shukri, even though he had graduated from Kadori, the same agricultural school where I graduated. Shukri led us to the nursery-garden and showed us how he was preparing the seedlings early in the year so as to let them grow well before the cold season : that enabled him to get flowers earlier than any gardener in the district.

'In this way we got the gold medal last year,' Shukri remarked, as he was stroking the small seedlings. He seemed to know everything on the farm. I had met many agriculturists, but I had not seen a man who spoke so confidently about the things he knew. When he spoke, it was in a loud, firm voice, with a smile that hardly ever left his face. In spite of our very short acquaintance, I liked him. Before we left, he proposed that he would look for a house for me if I wanted to stay in the village.

'Yes, please. Next week I will get my cases and I want to see the house before,' I said.

Two days later Shukri came and told me that he had found a separate room for me with a family who told him that they knew my parents. 'Om Muhamad is a good and kind woman. Her husband died many years ago. She is living just with her daughter and two sons. She promised to help you because she knows your mother well.'

I could not remember this woman, but I knew well the family name, among whom we had many friends. I agreed to go with him to have a look at the house, so Shukri told her youngest son that we were coming that day in the afternoon rest.

We found the small child waiting for us at the door. As he saw us coming he disappeared into the house, and before we could knock an old woman came out and said, 'You are welcome! Come! How is it you look for a house when we are here?'

She went on talking as we went upstairs to the room which was presumed to be mine. I found that it really was very clean and tidy. From the room I could see most of the village, because it was almost the highest one in the village. In front of the room and on the eastern side, there was an empty space surrounded by a low wall of old stones. On that wall there were three pots in which mint was growing. Inside the room there were a number of mattresses and quilts. Shortly after we entered it, a very beautiful girl with pretty, sad features came, carrying a tray with three cups of coffee. Om Muhamad introduced her to me as Nahielah, her daughter. The mother asked me not to bring anything with me and told me that I ought to regard myself as one of the family.

The next week I brought my few things. My mother had insisted on my taking them, even though she was sure the Om Muhamad her friend would not let me use any of them. She told me that she was one of the best women she knew. My mother was right, because most of the food I brought with me stayed unused. Om Muhamad's kindness let me feel at home in a very short time.

I got in touch with the people in the village through Shukri and Om Muhamad. There was a main street in the village, where were most of the shops and the only two coffee-shops. I used to pass through that street towards my room in Om Muhamad's house. During the day I spent my time at the school.

I used to get up early and take my breakfast, which would be already prepared either by Nahielah or her mother. Then I used to go to the school and play volley-ball with the students until the teachers arrived from the town at eight o'clock. In the afternoons I preferred to stay at school and have my dinner with the teachers. As soon as the classes ended, the teachers would leave for the bus, which might be already there, waiting for them at the gate (sometimes, feeling that they were late, the driver sounded his horn as an alarm). I used to stay until sunset with the boys, Shukri and some of the young men from the village, playing football and volley-ball.

Before leaving, Shukri would insist that I drink a cup of coffee with him. He made it himself, and Ahmad, the other doorkeeper, sometimes made a third for our group. Then I used to leave for the village, accompanied by a group of young men and the students. Then, after I reached the house, I did my corrections and prepared next day's lessons, and some nights I would play cards with Shukri and other men.

That was my daily programme until I heard that there were many pigeons near the village, when I began to get up earlier and to go out shooting just as the sun was rising. Mansor, a good old man, used to accompany me on my early exercise. I used to spend nearly two hours at it and come back to the school before the teachers could reach it. Sometimes Shukri came with me, and he used to cook any birds I might shoot.

Abu Alez was pleased when he saw me once bringing back eighteen pigeons, and I insisted on his taking some to his children. I could not forget how one day he had come to me in the garden, when I was working with the students, and showed me a great flock of pigeons which were quartering the plain near the school. He said that he would take over my duty if I went and shot some of them. But, seeing me ready to go, he smiled and was about to say something, when the birds flew up and went far away. I returned to work, and Abu Alez—that so strict and disciplined man—kept on looking after the birds, with his hands shading his eyes, till they disappeared behind the western hills. Sometimes I went shooting after the end of classes. Most times I did not return empty-handed.

I liked the people very much and I felt that they really had the same feeling for me. I was known among some of them as the bedouin teacher. They liked to call me so, and I liked it. No week passed without my being invited by one of the villagers. They made me feel at home among them, so I would not normally go to my family at the week-ends. They usually prepared interesting weekends. I tried to help them and I found Shukri to be of a great help in this.

We succeeded in improving some of the cultivation methods, but only to some extent. Some of my students started small projects—rabbit-breeding for example, or planting the newly introduced Marmont tomato—and they were successful, considering the limited resources they had. I helped these students within the facilities and authority I had. Many times I went with the farmers to their fields and saw how they simply planted in hope and waited for rain to water the land and bring up the seeds they had planted.

I liked staying in this good village among those nice and good-hearted people. I could not say that they were all angels : there were some evil ones in the village, but these were few and known by most of the people.

Two months passed before I was told one day by one of the students that a bedouin living near the village claimed that he knew me. The boy added, 'He may come today or tomorrow to see you.'

'Don't you know his name?'

'Yes, sir, he is just known as Abu Saleh.'

'Hasn't he any son in the school?'

'No, he hasn't. And I don't know if he has any at home or not.'

The next day, 'Afforestation Day', I was with a group of the boys digging some holes on that part of the hillside which belonged to the school, when Shukri, accompanied by a man, came up the small mountain. I tried to recognize the man, but I could not. He was smiling as he came near. Before they reached me, he turned his face towards Shukri and murmured a few words which I could neither understand nor guess. He was a tall man with small moustaches and a greyish beard. He was wearing a black robe, the usual dress for the bedouins and some villagers.

'Peace be with you,' the man said as he reached me. Before I could stretch out my hand to greet him, Shukri introduced him to me : 'This is Abu Saleh. He has come to see you.'

'Welcome, Abu Saleh. I was told by a boy, yesterday, that you would come.' The boys stopped working and gathered round the boy who had told me about Abu Saleh's visit. They were smiling a little. He might be telling them something about the man. I was sure of the bedouin's sensitiveness, so I looked at the boys and they went on with their work.

'I think that you do not remember me,' he said.

'I am sorry to say that I don't.' As I said these words I tried to recollect where I had seen that face and heard that voice. I felt that he was not completely strange to me. 'Perhaps I have met you, but I do not know when or where,' I added.

The man looked at Shukri, who was glancing from me to the man, then he turned his face to me and said, 'I am from your tribe. I am Ahmad Abu Lihiah. I knew you when you were a small child playing with the other boys in Wadi Al-Hisi. I know your father, mother and all your family except the small ones.'

I felt ashamed, because I knew many of Abu Lihiah's people and I knew a man of this name, but he was younger and a little different from the man standing in front of me reminding me of happy days passed. I was about to express my sorrow, when he continued, 'You are not to be blamed, my boy. You were too young when it was lost. It is land, and land only, that can keep people together.' As he spoke he pointed to the new-grown grass at our feet.

I asked him to sit and asked Shukri to make us a cup of tea. Abu Saleh agreed to sit, but excused himself from the tea-drinking. I answered all his enquiries. He was speaking about the people as if they were written on the grass in front of him. He made some comments on some names, either praising or joking.

I felt it was my turn to ask him about his family, and he told me that he had only a son and a daughter. He was afraid that they would grow up without knowing or being known to their relatives. Both of them were still children. I learnt that he was working as a guard for cornfields in the southern part of the village. He was living in a small old house about four miles to the south-west of the village.

I accepted willingly the invitation he offered, and promised to come the next Friday to have dinner with him. He bade me farewell and left. I had completely forgotten the boys and as I turned my face I saw that some were standing and others sitting, but the whole were listening to a talkative one who was, perhaps, telling a story.

The next Friday I went to visit Abu Saleh. As I reached the place I saw him standing with his two children in front of the small old house. When he saw me, he came to meet me, followed by a small boy of about five. He greeted me, and turned to the boy and said, 'This is Saleh, my son.'

I took the boy by his hand and followed the father to the house. The small girl left the doorway and went inside. Since it was a sunny day, he was putting an old carpet on the grass. 'I preferred this place because of the nice sun today,' he said.

We sat there. His wife soon came and made more enquiries than her husband, and complained of her loneliness in this distant house.

'We feel strangers here,' she said. 'The people here do not know our names. They just say, "The bedouins came", and "The bedouins went." That is life : sometimes it is sweet and other times it is bitter.'

The two children felt friendly with me and began to tell me about the games they had. They told me about their cousins who would come in the next few days and about the young deer which they had seen three days previously. They asked me to tell them stories as their father did, but they did not give me the chance to do so because they went on with their unbroken report.

'Here is one of your relatives who came to see you, Sara,' Abu Saleh said to his children.

'When will the others come, father?' the girl asked.

'In the coming few days,' he replied.

We had a very nice bedouin meal on the old carpet near the old small house, interrupted by some tales by Abu Saleh or by his children's questions. In the evening I left, and promised to come back when I had any opportunity.

When I went to my family I told my parents about Abu Saleh. They told me that he was one of the rich and good people before we were driven from Wadi Al-Hisi.

'I know him well,' said my father. 'He had more than one man to look after his cornfields and animals. That's why he tries to keep away from the people who knew him in Wadi Al-Hisi. He had no children when we were there. Poor Abu Saleh!'

My father sighed.

Last summer I was on my annual leave from my ministry job in Saudi Arabia. I felt that I had to pay a visit to Om Muhamad, the woman who had been kind to me for a full year, and to Abu Saleh in Samo. I do not know why I feel a great nostalgia for that village. It does not differ greatly from the other villages where I worked, but still I think more of it. There are many things in life for which one could not give an explanation if asked, and my love for that village, its people and hills, is one of these things.

When I decided to go, I bought a small gift for Om Muhamad and some toys and sweets for Abu Saleh's children, and went to the bus station. I found that the driver was the same one as in my time four years previously, and perhaps had been the driver for six or seven years before I came to the village. There were some men and women in the bus. I greeted them, and those who knew me came and shook hands, while some of the others whispered, perhaps asking about the stranger.

A few minutes later the bus moved off, and we left Hebron and passed through the full, ripe vineyards and orchards along the same road I had taken five years before. The bus was full. On the way, near one of the vineyards, the man who was sitting next me got down. Seeing the seat empty, the conductor came and sat by me. I knew his face, but I could not remember his name. He was from the village, but he had not been the conductor when I had been there. He seemed to know me, because he began to remind me of some events which happened while I was in the village. I asked him about the school and the villagers.

'All the people are the same as you left them. The old ones have died and the young ones have got married,' he said with a smile.

'How does life go with Om Mohamad?' I asked.

**173**

'She is well and her daughter got married and she has a child,' he said.

'I have heard about the heavy rain last winter and the bus-load that drowned. Can you tell me how it happened?'

He looked at his watch, then said, 'Let me first punch the tickets.' He left me and began to do his job. When he had finished his work he came and sat next me, got out a cigarette, lighted it and began to tell me the story.

'It was a rainy morning not different from any other. It was raining when most of the schoolboys came to the bus-station. We had two buses waiting in the station. A long discussion took place among the boys, whether to go that day or not. They decided to go because they had gone on worse days. I saw the girls coming to the bus slowly, as if they were unwilling to go. Few boys returned home, and we went with the others.

'We were just afraid of the low bridge near Karma, because of its being built on the greatest *wadi* in this district. As you know, it is a few miles on the western side of the village. We reached it soon. As we came to its eastern edge, the water was flowing over the whole valley, so we were unable to see the bridge.

'We stopped there and were divided into two camps: one said that we had to return because it was very dangerous to pass over an unseen bridge, while the other one, which included the driver, decided to cross—and the driver claimed that he knew the road well. We were unable to estimate the height of the water, because there was no sign of the bridge. In vain we tried to persuade the driver and his party not to cross the dangerous water-course. Seeing him obstinate, we all agreed, in spite of the great danger we felt, except two villagers who got out of the bus and waited on the bank. The bus went into the water. We all kept silent as the driver was moving the steering-wheel steadily.

' "Now we are on the bridge . . ." Before the driver could finish his sentence the bus had already leant over to the left, and soon it was completely in the water. I tried to get out and I opened one of the windows—the water rushed in, but I succeeded in getting on to the vehicle's roof, which was not reached by the water. Most of the others did the same, and the rest were forced to do so because the water was rushing fiercely into the bus. We dragged up the girls and small boys, and we all became stranded on a bus-roof in a wide, rushing torrent.

'The boys and girls began to look for each other, afraid of having forgotten someone inside—but all were there. We were frightened that the rain might increase and consequently the water would rise above the roof-rack and we would all be drowned. We looked at the sky : it was black on all sides and there was no hope of the rain stopping. The water was a little brown from the mud that it had. There were many strange things seen in the water, but it was too swift to recognize them. The driver stood silent, while the boys were still keeping their spirits up, and I thought it was just a matter of showing their bravery to the girls, who were shaking with fear. One of the two men whom we had left on the bank had already left for the village to bring help, while the other stood there to watch our fate.

'On the mountain at the southern side of the road there was the cornfield guard's house. The poor bedouin had been watching us and, when he saw what had happened, ran quickly down the mountain with his wife. His children ran behind him at first, but returned when they felt the heavy rain. I saw his wife return and then come back with something in her hands.

'It would take the man who was running to the village at least thirty minutes, and so we had to wait about an hour before the people could reach us. The rain was increasing and the water was increasing too, till it began to flow round our feet.

'The bedouin guard and his wife reached the man who stood on the bank. They had a rope with them. There were some rocks near them.

' "Don't be afraid!" the guard shouted. "I'll bring the rope and we'll get you out safe."

'He tied the rope to one of the rocks, took off his clothes and got down into the water, while his wife and the other man laid hold of the rope near the rock. In vain we tried to make him wait for the people, but he had already entered the water and begun to walk. He began to wade slowly in the stream. He was fighting against the current.

'The waves began to come up to his shoulders. He arrived near us, but we were unable to hear his voice over the thundering current. He began moving towards us very slowly, until he could move no more. The waves struck him, swept over his head. He looked towards us, then backwards at his wife and the other man, then up at his home on the hill. Perhaps he said something, but we could not make anything of his words. I saw him trying to move, but a great wave came over him and he lost his balance. He tried to swim, but the current was too strong. His wife and that other man began to haul on the rope, but in vain, for the current was stronger than them. The man was struggling, sometimes floating, then sinking. At last we saw him rushed away by the swift current and in a few seconds he was seen no more. His wife began running along the bank, but she could not find anything, and she too disappeared up the curves of the valley.

'The clouds were still black and the sky was still dark, too, when the villagers came in the second bus and on some of the trucks, with most of the people of the village in a long line behind them. They were unable to do anything, and they ordered us not to try because a group of policemen were coming from Hebron to our help. Soon the rain stopped and the policemen arrived in their Land-Rovers. One of these Land-Rovers was tied with an iron cable to a great winch. The Land-Rover, with its windows shut, entered the water and soon it was near our bus. Some of the boys were transferred to the car and it returned in reverse, helped by the winch, till it reached the other side. And so the action was repeated till we all were safe on the other side.'

'What was the end of the bedouin guard?' I asked.

'A week later, when some children were playing in the sands of a valley near Gaza on the Mediterranean shore, they saw a man's fingers sticking up from the sand and he was discovered to be Abu Saleh, the bedouin guard.'

'Don't you know anything about his wife and children?'

'They stayed on for about two weeks. Then they were taken by a bedouin who was said to be one of their relatives and from that time we have heard of them no more.'

At that moment we reached the bus-station and I got down. I followed the old lane to Om Muhamad's house, thinking what should I say about the children's gifts that I carried.